TEACHER TALES

Dennis,
Best regards,
Rich

TEACHER TALES

Richard Adelman

new texture

Contents

Contents

1. Mr. Kessler

AFTER I retired, I constructed a small writer's niche for myself in the large double closet that my wife used to use for her clothing. I am tapping on the keyboard of my laptop in this space right now. The closet is about two feet deep and maybe six feet wide. After I removed the poles that held the hangers, and the closet was empty, I made a small desk by laying a piece of plywood on two supports that I screwed into the walls. Very simple. There has always been a light in this closet, so I can close the sliding doors, and I never work longer than the battery in my laptop lasts, so I can shut the doors tight without running a wire to the electrical outlet outside. Generally, I start writing around nine in the morning. I am able to set my laptop on my simple desk, pull the cord of the fluorescent light, shut the doors completely, and write undisturbed and fully insulated for a blessed three hours. It's as though I am not even in my house, or in my city, but in a separate place altogether. Top to bottom, the walls and the ceiling of the closet are covered in elaborate wallpaper from the '40s, a design of large paisley flowers blooming on sinuous stems, and this otherworldly wallpaper reinforces the illusion of being somewhere else. After my writing has absorbed me for a few hours, the battery icon in the upper corner of the laptop screen gives me a red warning signal, and I know it's time to quit and take a drink.

I fabricated my writer's niche because I knew that in retirement I'd be bored, that my life would be empty, and I hoped that by writing, I could occupy my days with a pleasurable pastime that would fill the void left by work. Unfortunately, I soon found that I had not stolen enough of Mr. Wood's stories to keep me busy for long, and that I was incapable of producing any creative writing on my own. I'd hoped the transcribing of Wood's stories would furnish the content for my writing, and rewriting them would be a hobby for my retirement. So when I ran out of his material, I hit a wall, which was scary. I floundered for a while. Fortunately, I found I was able to produce one kind of writing: confession—that is, to just go ahead and tell the truth about myself—and I found that confession is, indeed, good for the soul. I needed to tell the truth—to confess (including the confession that I stole Mr. Wood's stories). Confession has made me feel a whole lot better about everything. Forcing myself to tell the truth, though not always pleasurable, has helped me cope with who I am. When you are alone in retirement and confronting yourself, believe me, you need a way to cope. So this story is as true as I could make it.

I was an English teacher in the public school system in Philadelphia for forty years. For all those years I kept a low profile. I minded my business, I covered my ass, and I didn't complain. I never asked a question—especially in a teachers' meeting, where a discussion might ensue. I always felt that discussion among teachers was counterproductive. I kept quiet throughout my career, and I taught my classes as my high school teachers had taught me. They understood that as long as a class is quiet and nothing is flying out of the windows, all is well. In a word, I stayed invisible, and this invisibility kept me out of trouble and helped me endure all those years. I might still be working except for a series of unfortunate incidents that compelled me to retire. In my fortieth year of teaching, I was beset by one troublesome event after another, until I was so rattled I jumped out of the teaching profession as though it were a burning building.

Actually the "burning building" is a faulty simile. Since I had accumulated forty years in the system, it wasn't as though my jump into retirement was dangerous. My pension was assured; with forty years under my belt, I could depend on a hundred percent of my final salary—a tidy sum—for the rest of my life.

On paper, I was ready to retire. But I didn't want to. I wanted to work until the end of the current contract—three more years—when I would be raking in an even tidier sum. Teaching, for me, had always been about the money, and the sum at the end of that contract—for life—was too good to pass up. But I found myself in a real jam in my fortieth year, and I jumped. Though my jump was more like running out of the ground floor of the burning building than jumping from a dangerous height.

Working in a large urban school district, a teacher expects a certain amount of stress. For forty years I accepted the anxieties and daily emotional upsets that teachers are heir to because they were part of the package for which the District paid me. I just wasn't prepared for the jolt I had in my last year.

Teachers live lives of continuous anxiety. They are squeezed in the jaws of a vise between the school's administration and its students, the boss and the customers. Students provide a continuous threat of disorder, and administrators make incessant, ridiculous demands.

In September, when the cicadas are screaming in the trees and there is a feeling of sadness in the air—right around Labor Day, which is a dreadful holiday for teachers—I often had a certain dream, a nightmare, that foretold the anxiety of the approaching school year. (I have compared my September nightmares with the nightmares of other teachers, and I can assure you that I am not alone in this. All teachers have a similar dream in autumn.) I remember the nightmare I had the night before the first day of my fortieth year. It went like this: I came to school in the darkness of the early morning, before the lights in the hallway were on. It was so dark, as I walked down the hall, I could not see a chair in front of me and fell over it. A swarm of mice skittered away on the terrazzo floor. I felt my way to my classroom by touching the walls. There, I switched on the light, and I was surprised to find that there was a large puddle in the middle of the room, deep as a pond. So deep, the chairs were floating on the surface, and the dark water swayed uneasily like water in a rocking bucket. The room had grown to twice its normal size. Looking up to find the source of the water, I saw rain falling right through the ceiling (even though my room was on the first of three stories, and it wasn't raining when I entered the building). The roof was like a porous old barn's, just bare laths. Like some character from Kafka, I thought, *Oh dear, how will I get ready for first period?* Besides the floating chairs, all kinds of debris floated in the puddle: books, board erasers, tea bags, scarves, sponges—all the flotsam of a classroom. There may have been some living things swimming in there too—a snake or something. The window was wide open, the glass was broken, and a chilly wind disturbed the water. I noticed, in the far corner of the room, near the open window, there was a student I recognized as Brendan, a sullen youth. He sat in the shallow water at the edge of the puddle smoking a cigarette. His hat was cocked over one eye. There was something glinting in his hand, perhaps a shard of glass. "Brendan," I said, "there's no smoking in school." At this, Brendan raised his cigarette to his lips and took a long, leisurely drag; then he flung the butt into the water and rose from his sitting position. The glass in his hand gleamed. Now I saw that many cigarette butts floated in the dirty puddle, along with a tire, and a shopping cart; and the puddle had an ugly edge of algae and smelled stagnant while it moved. For a moment, I thought Brendan would come my way and meant to harm me with his broken glass. But instead, he screeched like a cat and clambered out the open window. Outside I heard the caterwauling of many cats, and the rain poured down in torrents, and the water sloshed against the walls of my enormous classroom. I waded into the forbidding pond, toward my floating desk, looking at the clock, understanding that the room must be ready in an hour for the school day. And I awoke.

I had a similar dream at the beginning of each of the forty years I was a teacher, and it reveals the way the job fills a teacher with unease.

However, in the year of my retirement, my teacher-anxiety increased to a level of panic, and I separated from the School District.

During my long career, I taught in two schools. For thirty years I was in Hubert Humphrey Junior High School in the northeast part of the city, and then I transferred to Northwest High School, which is the site of this story. I started at Humphrey Junior High so long ago, I actually remember Senator Humphrey himself visiting the school as part of his presidential campaign back in 1968, and I remember the fuss the school made about his visit, hanging buntings and flying flags at the front of the building and using the steps of the school for dignitaries and security personnel, while all the students and faculty and visitors, including the press, stood and faced the front of the school to listen to the august liberal speechify about the importance of education to democracy. He sure could get worked up. I was a Republican, though, always have been, and I voted for the maliciously maligned and disgraced Richard Nixon, who was actually a great peacemaker and humanitarian.

I transferred to Northwest High School because it was, and still is, an academic magnet school, meaning they restrict their admissions to students with better grades and attendance. My seniority in the system assured my transfer, and I thought it would be easier and more pleasant to teach in a school where the students had higher levels of achievement. I was tired of teaching those slugs at Humphrey. And I was getting too old to chase twelve-year-olds around the room.

Unfortunately I'd gotten a bit spoiled at Humphrey, and when I came to Northwest, I had a little trouble continuing certain practices I'd gotten used to. At Humphrey, so few students actually did assignments, there was precious little to grade. I never had any trouble finishing all my grading during the school day. Consequently, I never, in all my time at Humphrey, took any work home with me. I had my evenings to myself, and rightfully so; after all, at the end of the school day, I was off the clock. When I came to Northwest, however, I found that if I were to do the job the school expected, I'd have to work in the evenings—grading papers—and I wasn't about to start doing that.

The problem was writing assignments—essays—that take forever to grade. At Humphrey, students didn't do them, but when I arrived at Northwest and realized that the students actually *did* their essays if I assigned them, I was horrified. I saw my colleagues hauling stacks of student essays home—sometimes in rolling suitcases—and I couldn't let that happen to me. I wasn't about to bring a briefcase full of student writing home. Never. So I stopped giving writing assignments altogether. And this was fine with my students. They had plenty of work to do for other classes, and they considered the light load from my class a boon. I assigned no written work while I taught at Northwest, and this assured my evenings would be my own.

I did make a show of taking work home by carrying a

briefcase in and out of the building every day—it would have been conspicuous at Northwest if I didn't—but the case held only my lunch and a magazine in case I had an idle moment.

Instead of written work I gave my students scores of objective tests. Objective tests—multiple-choice, true-or-false, and the like—were easy to score, and they provided me with loads of grades at the end of a report period to justify a student's progress. Giving this kind of test exclusively may not have been in keeping with the school's policy, but how could they complain when their never-ending batteries of school-wide and nationwide tests were also objective tests? I was doing my students a favor by giving them plenty of practice in this kind of test. Neither my students nor I missed those laborious essay assignments.

Since I am determined to tell the whole story of my final year in teaching, even the hard parts, I'll explain why I needed my evenings free. The reason was that I had (have) a mild drinking problem—mild in that I have never drunk as much as I reckon a full-fledged alcoholic drinks, but a problem nevertheless since I have spent every evening for as long as I can remember in an alcoholic haze, and my ritual of drinking after work, I always thought, was as essential to my survival at school as food or sleep. During my career, I generally drank two generous martinis in the course of an evening (five or six ounces of gin altogether), and I performed this ritual nightly from the day I started working. It was my habit to begin drinking the moment I returned home from work, and then to drink throughout dinner, sinking deeper and deeper into a muddle and, once I achieved the required level of alcohol-induced anesthesia, I watched television for the rest of the night. I was always too drunk to understand the evening news, but I dearly loved the ubiquitous detective programs that came on later, especially the ones where the detective was quirky or neurotic or antisocial.

I think you can see why I was indisposed to take work home from school. I was busy.

I have to go a bit deeper still. I was never really cut out to be a teacher, and I should have settled on something else. From the day I started teaching until my last day, I was sick—literally sick. Throughout my career, I suffered from ailments that haunted me almost every day I taught. I had a breathing problem, and sometimes I struggled to breathe all day, until by last period I was dizzy and frightened and unable to catch my breath. At the same time, I experienced an irregular heartbeat. I'd get exhausted by about third or fourth period, depending on how active I was, and my heart would sort of hesitate, then race, sometimes a dozen times a day. At the same time, I was the victim of intense esophageal cramps, which felt like some demon was stabbing me in the middle of my chest with a long hatpin. Combined with my shortness of breath and irregular heartbeats, these cramps made me, on many occasions, sure I was having a heart attack. And these attacks would happen invariably while I was in front of a class, teaching, and I just had to pretend the symptoms weren't there and work through them. My students would see a nervous, perspiring old man, but I'm sure they thought nothing of it. They were used to adults acting in odd ways and couldn't care less.

I didn't let these symptoms go untreated. I was a regular in the offices of a few doctors. My family doctor was the most perspicacious. I would visit him a few times a year, when my symptoms were most pronounced, and he'd send me for a number of annoying tests—X-rays, stress tests, breathing tests, MRIs, blood work—all kinds of tests. If the tests were inconclusive, as they usually were, he'd send me to a specialist who might order a few more tests. The business of confessing my ailments to these doctors and undergoing the rigors of the tests, combined with the expiation of waiting nervously for the results, always cured my symptoms. Soon after a visit to a specialist or a round of medical tests, my symptoms would magically disappear—for a while. I don't know if my family doctor pursued all this testing to shield himself from indemnity, thinking if I were really sick and he let it slip by, he'd be in a jam, or if he considered the tests a form of therapy for me, or both. But they were effective in alleviating my symptoms, though never curing whatever it was that made me sick.

Incredibly, when I retired I had over two hundred days in my sick-leave bank, indicating that I used very few sick days during my career. I somehow worked through the pain. I guess there was really very little wrong with me. All the tests I'd taken over the years for all the ailments that plagued me came back negative—every one. A cardiologist gave me some blood pressure medicine that regulated my heartbeat, and that was the extent of any therapy I ever needed—beyond confession and extensive testing. I guess confession has always done me good.

I can only conclude that the teaching job made me psychosomatically sick. Once home, ailing from a day of teaching, I sought relief in the form of a frosty martini, my medicine of choice, and it worked wonders. I never mentioned this regime of self-medication to any doctor, though, for fear he would ask me to discontinue the practice, and I believe I would sooner have discontinued the practice of visiting the doctor than discontinue the practice of drinking martinis.

In my retirement year, my physical symptoms exploded—due, I expect, to the misfortunes I encountered—and of course I had to ratchet up the level of self-medication. All of which helped precipitate my departure from the job.

2. I am displaced

My LAST year, during third period, my lunch period, when I normally had my room to myself, a hitch in my roster forced me to eat lunch in the English office across the hall instead of in my own room, because a "floating" teacher, Miss Rigg, came into my room that period and displaced me. In previous years I could spread out during third period. I could eat a leisurely lunch, read a magazine, do some paperwork, straighten the room—do whatever was necessary. I had the whole room to myself; no one bothered me. I could close the door and be invisible. I can't tell you how my heart sank the first day of the year when Miss Rigg and a group of her students, eleventh graders, invaded my room when I was about to eat lunch and relax.

"I'm your new roomie," piped young Miss Rigg, steering a cart full of papers and books into the room. Her flimsy dress and unrestrained hair showed how lately the summer had ended. She beamed and pointed toward the front of the room. "Can I use this section of the chalkboard?"

"I suppose so," I said, and I felt the first stirrings of anxiety.

A floating teacher is a teacher without a room of her own, who must encamp throughout the day in other teachers' rooms. She wheels her cart full of supplies—her portable classroom—into the room of a teacher who has the period free, followed by a swarm of noisy teenagers, and the regular occupant (in this case me) needs to find a place to bivouac. So, from that first day on, when the floating teacher entered my room, I hastily gathered my things— my banana, my apple, my snack bar, my computer, and some papers to grade—and I retreated to the English office—with every intention of doing what I would normally do in my own room. And that's how I got to know Mr. Wood and Mrs. Worthington. We met every third period in the small English department office and had lunch together. At first I kept to myself while I ate my meager lunch, but after a while I found myself in idle conversation with my new friends.

The English office was as crowded as an antique shop. It was primarily the office of Mrs. Hegel, the department chair. She organized the department's business on the top of her desk using piles of papers, stacked one atop another, crosswise, to distinguish one pile from the next. These piles grew higher and higher—I have no idea what they contained—and there were quite a few of them, so that the actual work area on her desk was a small one-foot square, just enough space to set down a paper and scribble a signature. These paper piles of Hegel's accumulated as the year went by and, once they reached the tipping point on her desk, they migrated to the window sill, the top of her file cabinet, her computer table, and a rolling cart that she brought into the office to accommodate the overflow. Finally these towering stacks began to reproduce on the teachers' worktable, which might otherwise seat three or four teachers comfortably were it not for the towers. My lunchmates and I sat at this table, and at times I could only see them from the chin up. The office also housed the department's photocopy machine, which produced its own stacks of papers—the mistakes and extras that hurried teachers discarded, along with the reams and reams of blank sheets waiting to be used. Also, the office was the hub for sets of books that teachers returned after borrowing them to distribute to their students. Piles of *The Iliad* teetered next to piles of *The Catcher in the Rye* and collapsed into towers of *Brave New World*. These stacks of books were piled on file cabinets that held the department's archives of tests on all these works of literature (which I never used, since the answer sheets were always missing). Finally, the room was surrounded on three sides by dusty bookshelves that held all manner of educational relics: reference books, old VHS tapes, sample copies of texts from vendors, and some antique tomes that a rare book dealer might find interesting. I once brought down a copy of *The Innocents Abroad* that had only one copyright date. Since I was alone in the office when I found this antique, I slipped it into my briefcase and added it to my personal library at home, knowing no one would notice it missing.

I think you can see how crowded the room was, but Chairwoman Hegel's husband applied the finishing touch to the décor by moving his desk into the cramped office. Although he was a social studies teacher, his affection and allegiance to his wife compelled him to take up residence next to her with a facing desk, and he used the same filing system as she—stacks of crisscrossed papers. Additionally, he was a devotee of the hands-on approach to teaching history; that is, he assigned his students the making of historical models and dioramas. His corner of the office was crowded with reproductions of famous icons that his students generated—the Wright Brothers' Flyer, the Roman Coliseum, knights in shining armor, Viking ships—and these, like all the papers and books, multiplied around the room as the year progressed, some of them produced by desperate students more adept at crafts than scholarship, who hoped to improve their grades by increasing the size of their models, until their efforts were almost life-sized. Yes, a life-sized sarcophagus of King Tut would not have surprised us if we saw it propped in the corner of the room behind Mr. Hegel's desk.

It was close quarters in that office, and dust lay everywhere. On the odd occasion when Mr. Hegel drew the ancient curtains that hung beside the windows, motes of dust as thick as schools of minnows swam through the shafts of light.

Luckily, during the period when my colleagues and I ate lunch, Mr. and Mrs. Hegel had classes to teach, so we were able to sit at the worktable and chat unsupervised. The Hegels were always eager to socialize with whomever they hosted in their office and, pulling rank, they were apt to hold court from the superior position of their desks and dominate the discussion. But the cat was away during this period, so we mice could do as we pleased.

Mr. Wood was somewhere past the middle of his career, in his forties, I guessed. A bit shabby, he wore jeans with a sport jacket and a buttoned-down shirt. He was getting to the age when a person needs to come to terms with the reality that his metabolism cannot cope with all the calories he consumes. His clothes were getting tight around the middle. Destined for baldness, he let his blond hair grow long, though not like a vagabond, more like a man who told his barber he was opting for long hair, and he combed it straight back. In his face I could see he had once been handsome; he had a definable jaw and a sparkle in his eye.

At the beginning, when Wood and I sat across the table from one another and said little, I knew him only by the surprising lunches he brought. These lunches denied his lapsed youth. He was partial to processed meats, combined with cheese, on white bread. He liked a hoagie from the Wawa or a cheesesteak from the truck down the street; there was ham (with a variety of spicy edges) combined with fragrant cheeses, and there was bologna and American with mayo, even liverwurst and onion. I was a little jealous, I must admit, because I remembered the time, long ago, when I would enjoy such lunches, before my doctors outlawed them and Mrs. Kessler stopped preparing them. For the last twenty years of my career, my lunch consisted of the same three items: a banana, an apple, and a snack bar (thank God for the luxury of the snack bar or I think I'd have gone insane). But Wood ate without restrictions. His chips were the high octane variety— deep fried in trans fat, not baked.

One day early in the year, as I was scoring tests, Mr. Wood unwrapped his lunch, and I was unsure what kind of sandwich he had, though I scrutinized it carefully, as usual. It had a familiar aroma.

"What's for lunch, Mr. Wood?" I asked.

Studying the edge of the sandwich, Wood replied, "Lebanon bologna and some kind of cheese." He dug in.

This sent me reeling. As I bit into my banana, I recalled the pleasures I had taken years ago with this same salty delicacy, so fatty and piquant. "I used to combine Lebanon bologna with cream cheese," I said, "And I would vary the types of cream cheese. I remember it was particularly good with chive cream cheese," and when I said this I felt the kind of tingle a boy feels when he sees a girl in clothes he likes. I resolved to stop at the supermarket on the way home and get a quarter pound of Lebanon bologna and a tub of cream cheese and eat it that very night. But I didn't.

"Hmm, sounds good," said Wood. "I might just try that."

Every day Mr. Wood unwrapped his lunch and filled the cluttered office with the aromas of garlicky cold cuts, with onions

sprinkled with oregano and soaked in oil, and various cheeses—
cheddar, Havarti, provolone—while I brooded on a diet of fruit
and paperwork.

Usually, young Mrs. Worthington joined us for lunch. She
ate a big salad, swimming in creamy dressings of every color,
from a Tupperware container. But she often didn't stay for the
whole period, unless Mr. Wood had launched into one of his
stories, which were irresistible. Worthington was younger than
we and had important work to do in the school. Although she
was a teacher, she had acquired administrative duties, owing no
doubt to her youth, her charm, her exuberance for her job, and
her recent schooling in all the modern methods of education.
She was lithe and energetic, dressed in tailored pinstriped suits—
seemingly never the same suit twice, nor the same silk shirt, nor
the same necklace (how did she do that?). She wore her hair in a
short, natural Afro, which suited the efficiency she needed for her
ambitious pursuits. She was on all kinds of committees and action
groups—a real go-getter, and a reliable resource for Mr. Wood,
who never read a memo and would never have known what was
due or what was going on in the school without her. When she sat,
she introduced a welcome whiff of lilies to the room—until she
pried open her Tupperware.

Thinking back, my greatest regret was what happened
between Mrs. Worthington and me, although I made a mess of
my friendship with Mr. Wood, too.

Our first real conversation—other than about food or memos—
resulted from Wood's saying something that I found particularly
annoying. He launched into a lengthy explanation about how he
planned to approach the next novel he planned to teach. My belief
always was that teachers should not share ideas. Everyone knows
what works for him, I thought, so it is counterproductive to hear
the ideas of others. I always hated when a colleague wanted to
discuss his teaching methods. I cringed when a fellow teacher
at a teachers' meeting would raise his hand and start in with the
words "What I do is...." I always wished such palaverers would
just shut up. Not only did no one care what the know-it-all had
to say, but the objective of a teachers' meeting has always been
to get it finished as swiftly as possible, and I did not appreciate
any unnecessary nattering, like questions and suggestions. I often
closed my eyes during meetings and, if I were lucky, drifted off to

sleep.

To my mind, Mr. Wood was breaking one of the cardinal rules of teacher interaction by talking about curriculum at lunch, and this gave me a negative early impression of him. He looked up from his Jewish salami sandwich, which may or may not have been on a twisted roll, and he asked, "Do you teach *The Color Purple?*"

"Yes," I said, "I teach it every year."

"You know," he said, swallowing and licking a bit of mustard from his thumb, "I think Alice Walker made this book too easy. The moral reasoning in *The Color Purple* is too clear. There's good and there's bad. But nothing in life is that clear. I've been thinking that I will present the idea that *The Color Purple* is an example of a novel that deconstructs commonly held beliefs. I think I can show how the book deconstructs myths—myths about women, and blacks, and even ugly people. Then we can work with the idea of deconstruction rather than the text. Deconstruction itself will be the focus. I can't deal with a book that depicts such moral clarity."

"What's the matter with clarity?" I asked, though I should have said nothing. Saying nothing is the best way to thwart a conversation. But I joined in, "I have taught *The Color Purple* for years," I said. "The kids like it. It's a book about an underdog who winds up on top. What's wrong with that? Guy beats up girl; guy gets his comeuppance. It's a book about a bully. The bully should always get it in the end. Pretty clear, no?"

"There is some moral ambiguity in the character of Shug. She's a righteous sinner," said Worthington, packing her briefcase and preparing to leave, "but if I taught *The Color Purple* I'd concentrate on the social issues. I think the social issues in the book *are* morally unambiguous but worth getting into."

Mercifully, Wood resumed ruminating on his idea of deconstruction (whatever that is) silently. His salami sandwich, I noted, looked like it contained slices that he actually cut from a miniature salami. "Sometimes the best parts of the book are in the subtexts," he mused. And I thought, *Poor kids. I'm glad I'm not in that class. What the hell are subtexts?* But I said, "You should go with that deconstruction thing. I think it will go well."

3. A confession elicits a story

As THE school year progressed, we blabbed more and more at lunch. We talked about small matters mainly: school gossip, movies, things in the news—nothing important, just distracting banter—until, after a while, I left my computer and all of the papers I planned to grade back in my room, and I showed up in the English office with only my lunch, ready for conversation. There was always a copy of *The New York Times* on the worktable, and Mr. Wood read it. He was furious with the Republican Party for, as he put it, "creating an agenda, not around issues, but around defeating its enemies," which I thought was a silly criticism since a political party can only succeed if it defeats its enemies, and the Republican party had always seemed to me the only party willing to tell the truth about issues like welfare and taxes; namely, that taxpayers do not like paying for welfare.

Wood might say, "It doesn't matter if Obama is right or wrong, the Republicans know they can score points with voters by opposing him."

And Worthington would agree, saying, "I guess we know why."

And I thought, *Obama is a socialist who wants to put his hands in my pockets to feed the so-called underprivileged,* but, not wishing to stir any controversy and trying to stall the conversation, I would say, "He sure has his hands full. Let's see what happens."

One morning, while I was finishing a snack bar, and Mr. Wood was working assiduously on some pungent Italian cold cut (mortadella I think), he asked Mrs. Worthington and me a question about discipline. "Do you think detentions work?"

Since the subject of discipline was the shop talk I most loathed, I recoiled. *Oh, brother,* I thought. *Here we go....* Throughout my career, the disciplining of students was the thing I resented most about the job of teaching. I never considered the behavior of students to be my responsibility. Their misbehavior was the fault of their parents, and responsibility for correcting this misbehavior should fall to their parents or the administration of the school, leaving teachers free to teach. About Mr. Wood's question concerning detentions, I thought, *Detentions! What teacher in his right mind would subject himself to the extra time after school that giving a detention would require of him? Only a sap gives a student a detention.* But to be sociable, I said, "Sure, they work. Give a detention."

"I have a student who is a real clown," Wood continued, "always after attention. The other day he got up from his seat, right in the middle of class, and he threw open the window and hollered something to a friend on the lawn. When the class settled, I asked him to see me after class, and I gave him a detention, which he attended. But it didn't do much good. Today he practiced shooting balled-up papers into the trash can. At least three times—during class, while I was talking—paper balls, flying through the air."

"So what did you do this time?" asked Mrs. Worthington.

"I gave him another detention."

"The little bastard. Write him up," I said. I was referring to the disciplinary form a teacher uses to refer a student to a disciplinarian. Why should Mr. Wood have to suffer these indignities when the school had, ostensibly, an expert—the disciplinarian—to take care of such cases?

Worthington shifted uneasily at my suggestion.

"This time I'll make him sit a bit longer," Wood continued. "Y'know, I have always depended on the interest level of my lessons to keep order...."

Was I hearing correctly? Did Wood say he depended on the interest level of his lessons to maintain order in his class? I thought, *Who's got a hundred and eighty hours of interesting lessons? Wood must really think highly of himself, and I doubt his students are of the same opinion. When it comes to discipline, surely threats are more effective than interest.* But not to seem obtuse, I said, "It's true. Students who are interested are far less likely to misbehave."

"...But it doesn't always work," continued Wood. "I guess I'm not always interesting...."

I nodded and smiled.

Worthington said, "You need to have a talk with this child."

Now, Worthington was a solid disciplinarian. I'd seen her in the hallway dressing down an unlucky pupil on more than one occasion. She'd be right in the miscreant's face, staring him into submission like a snake charmer and lecturing him like a displeased mother. When the mischief-maker looked away, Worthington turned his chin back to her with her finger—actually touched him—so he would maintain eye contact. She could give a proper scolding.

"Yes," said Wood, "I will speak with him."

I thought, *Right. You'll speak with him. Good one. I doubted that Wood could perform the snake-charming routine. Worthington could get away with it because she was a woman and black, and black women are a lot scarier than white men, especially white men with blue jeans and long hair.* But to be positive and ingratiating, I said, "Excellent idea, have a talk with him."

"Or call his mom," said Worthington. "Some of these guys have very effective parents."

And I thought, *Call his mom! Oh, rue the day! A call to a parent could take up an entire period. Parents love to blab about their children, even if the teacher has called to tell them bad things. Before you know it they're going into details about the kid's whole life, offering defenses and mitigating circumstances, giving a medical history.... Just write the kid up. Let someone else take care of the problem—a counselor or a disciplinarian. Or just forget it.* But knowing this to be a popular remedy for misbehavior, I said, "Yes, good idea, call the parent."

Wood ruminated. Worthington resumed grading the essays that lay in a pile before her.

Then, something bubbled up from inside me, and I said something unusual, for me. It must have been this conversation about discipline, transpiring among people I'd grown to trust, that prompted me to say, "I've been having an annoying problem in my class that's driving me crazy."

"And for you that's a short ride," joked Wood.

"Yes. Well, it's like this: Someone, I don't know who, has been stealing things from my desk. At first it was little things, like the staple-remover and batteries, and lots of pens, all kinds of pens and things, whatever I left in the drawer, even paper clips."

"You *noticed* that paper clips were missing?" Worthington wondered.

"Yes, because he—or she—took them all. I can't lock the desk because there is no key. All I can do is move everything to the closet, which is very inconvenient. But whatever I leave in the drawer turns up missing. One morning I opened the drawer and found that a little flash drive was missing. I put it in the drawer the day before. It had a backup copy of all the tests I have given this year and God-knows what else."

"Oh, no!" said Wood. "All your tests are—out there?"

Worthington, mouth open, stared at me in disbelief.

"Yes," I said, "and there's more: Someone—perhaps the same perpetrator—is hiding things from me. He—or she—hid the board erasers—put them under one of the desks; and he hid my pointer—put it behind the file cabinet. This trickster moves things all around the room—moved the teachers' edition of the textbook to the windowsill in the back of the room. I've been spending countless hours retrieving things. It's driving me nuts."

"Sounds like you've got an enemy," said Worthington. "Did you make anyone angry?"

"Not that I know of. I mean, nothing out of the usual. Students are always upset about something."

Wood seemed interested. "Hmmmm," he said, "you're always in the room, are you?"

"Yes," I said, "this period is the only period I'm not in there. Miss Rigg uses the room this period. And I lock the room over night. Only the cleaning person goes in, and he has better things to do, I think, than hide the board erasers."

"Then your crook is striking this period...right now, as we speak..." said Wood. "Who do *you* think is doing it? Usually the person you *think* is the culprit *is* the culprit."

"Are you kidding?" Worthington chuckled. "Usually the person you *don't* think is the culprit is the culprit."

"I'm suspicious of a guy named Brendan in my fourth period class, but he'd have to be awfully clever to get away with it, because he would be stealing right under my nose. To be honest, I have no idea who's doing it. But it's driving me to drink."

"And for you, that's a sh—"

"Don't say it."

This thievery *was* really bothering me. Whoever wanted to get into my head and do mischief was succeeding. I checked my drawers constantly, and I arranged things in deliberate ways to make sure nothing was moved. I even thought of putting a mousetrap in the drawer, though I knew I'd be the one to trip it. When I came back from an errand around the school, I jumped into my empty room, and said "Ah ha!" in an effort to surprise the crook. When I found something lost or hidden, I felt humiliated. I spent considerable time searching and cursing.

"Kids are a mystery," said Wood.

"They need boundaries," said Worthington.

"I hate them," I said. "School would be so much better without them."

Wood leaned back in his chair and crossed his legs at the ankles, as though he meant to relax and perhaps pursue my problem further, but instead he launched into an incredible story. Speaking in a matter-of-fact tone which he maintained throughout the tale, he began by telling us that his previous teaching assignment was in Charles Wilson Peale High School in the southern part of the city. In that school, he claimed, the principal wanted to standardize classroom discipline and to have a uniform method of implementing this discipline. So the principal installed in every classroom a disciplinary system that would dole out rewards and punishments at the press of a button. This system was a "technological wonder," said Wood. It included a panel, which looked like the panel a sound technician might use, and this panel sat on the teacher's desk and replicated the seating arrangement in the room. Each seat in the classroom had a corresponding box on the panel, and in this box there was a red button and a green button. Now, the whole room was electrified, so if the teacher pushed the red button, the student in the corresponding seat would get an electric shock and scream "Ouch!" But—and here comes the part that made us giggle, though Wood remained impassive—if the teacher pushed the green button, the student in the corresponding seat would receive a delicious sensation that would pervade his or her whole body and make him or her squirm with delight, *"Ooooo!"* (Worthington and I found this especially funny because Wood slipped out of character for a moment and enacted the squirm and the *Ooooo.*) Wood went on to explain how the principal issued a directive, stating exactly when the buttons should be employed and how long the duration of the sensation should last, since by keeping the button pressed the teacher could extend the shock or burst of pleasure for a length of time. If a student answered a question correctly, he enjoyed a shot of pleasure. If a student talked out of turn or committed some other offense, he received a painful blast of electricity. If a student asked a provocative question that evinced, as Wood put it, "higher order thinking skills," he earned a prolonged sensation of pleasure; just as, Wood explained, if a student did something egregious, he would be electrocuted.... And this, by the principal's measure, would provide the school with a fair, effective means of discipline at the fingertips, you might say, of the staff.

Unfortunately, Wood explained, the system went haywire. He related how the bad kids, after a number of shocks, refused to sit down and stood up throughout the class; how angry the students were after being shocked, and how they made ugly threats; how confusion reigned when students started begging for pleasure, and how many hands shot up to answer a question with any old answer just hoping to get a nice *Ooooo.* He went on to explain how male teachers tended to give more sensations of pleasure to female students—and longer sensations, sometimes obscenely long. And how they gave more electric shocks to male students, and how surprising it was that female teachers did the same— gave more shocks to males; and how some races received more shocks than others ("Um hm," said Worthington); and how some cynical teachers gave nothing but shocks; and how some bleeding heart optimists gave only sensations of pleasure. "It was just a mess," said Wood.

Wood ended the story by explaining how he discovered that his own teacher's chair was wired by the administration and they could apply pain or pleasure to him. He said he was teaching a lesson on the parts of speech, and he was reviewing a drill. The students were going up and down the rows giving their answers, and he was pressing the green button and delivering a short *Ooooo* if the student responded correctly, and he was doling out an *Ouch* if the student answered an item wrong. Then, suddenly he felt a shock, and he jumped out of his seat and screeched, "Ouch, damn it!" which made the whole class roar with laughter (not unlike Worthington and I, who thought this was hilarious). Wood said he received a memo later in the day explaining how the administration frowned on the teaching of the parts of speech, and he could spend his time more productively by teaching "critical thinking skills."

"Anyhow," Wood concluded, "the dispensation of pain or pleasure was never consistent, neither for students nor for teachers, and all sorts of biases ruled, so this experiment in maintaining classroom order ended in classroom chaos, and the whole expensive system had to be dismantled."

Worthington and I were speechless. Incredulous, we looked first at each other, then at Wood.

"No lie," said Wood, poker-faced.

Although my breathing problem was acting up, and I should have headed for the teachers' lounge for a nap, later that day, during my preparation period, while Wood was teaching a class of twelfth graders, I felt the need to pop by his classroom and run something by him concerning my problem with thievery. More than that, I wanted to eavesdrop on him. I wanted to see how that method of maintaining-order-by-keeping-things-interesting was working out for him. Actually, I hoped to find his class in a state of chaos, which would disprove his theory and make me feel better about myself. I was, however, disappointed to find that his students were not misbehaving. There were no sleepers, no text messengers, no daydreamers, no chatterers, and no idlers as there were in my own twelfth grade classes. I decided Wood must have a good class during this particular period, but this thought barely kept me from succumbing to a feeling of jealousy.

Wood seemed to be working very hard, though, and that made me feel better. I would be winded and suffer heart palpitations by second period if I expended the kind of energy he was expending— and it was already sixth period, by which time I would be dead if I jumped around the room the way he was. The whole time I watched, he stood on his hind legs and showed things on his projector; he explained things lengthily and gave directions *ad nauseam*. And he milled about, keeping his eye on what students were up to—even when they were hard at work. Why did he need to get out of his chair if his students were busy? The whole point of getting students busy is to take a break and catch your breath.

During the class the difference between the verbs "lie" and "lay" came up, and Wood explained the difference. I admit he explained the difference well, beginning with the confusion arising from the similarity between "to lay," the infinitive, and "lay," the past tense of "lie." When he had finished the basics, as a joke, he said, "And the whole thing is complicated by the slang version of 'laid,' as in 'Tony laid the girl in the back seat of the car.'" With this Wood stopped by the desk of the student who obviously was Tony, a thin, swarthy youth with a huge shock of black hair, and touched his shoulder, continuing, "But as we all know, if Tony laid the girl in the back seat of a car, it's probably because she's dead, and someone in his family has asked him to dispose of her—so he laid her in the back seat." And throughout this routine, Wood's students laughed as though they were sitting in a comedy club—which put my nose out of joint, since if I told a dirty joke or an ethnic joke in my class, my students would crucify me. Why did he get away with it?

I actually bumped into Wood at his doorway while I was eavesdropping—*What was he doing near his door?*—and he acted as though he knew I was there the whole time. "Hello, Kessler," he said, casually, as if he had bumped into me on the street. He was extracting a square caramel from its wrapper.

"I was just rearranging some things in my briefcase," I said. I'd laid my briefcase on the heat register outside his door.

But he was unconcerned with my excuse. He popped the caramel in his mouth.

"Listen," I said, "I've been thinking about my problem with the thief, and I'm sure you're right. It's happening while we're eating lunch. Rigg is a new teacher and wouldn't know if something was happening right under her nose. So here's what I want to do: I want to set up a video camera in the room and do some surveillance. If I put the camera on a tripod and aim it right at my desk during third period and start recording, it wouldn't look like it's on. It would look like it's just standing there. If the thief is striking during third period, I'll find him. Neither Rigg nor her students will ever know the difference."

Remarkably, Wood's class did not veer out of control while I had his attention. He said, "I have a video camera. You get the tapes and you can use my camera. Get MiniDV tapes. MiniDV. And leave the rest to me. I have a tripod too." Then Wood wheeled around and resumed his lesson. "OK class, time to talk about the concept of *deus ex machina*," he said.

Deus ex machina! Can you imagine? What the hell is *deus ex machina?* I wrote "MiniDV" on the back of the magazine in my briefcase.

4. A tale of two students

As THE weather grew cooler, the English office became more inviting. The heat register in my room worked poorly, and the temperature in the morning felt as though it was just as cold indoors as out; while in the English office, right across the hall, the temperature was balmy all the time. Ours was an old building, and the heating plant had been modified a few times. There was steam heat in some rooms and forced air in others, and some rooms had both, and often both worked equally poorly. But the English office was nice and cozy in winter, even while the rest of the building was frigid. As the days shortened and Chairwoman Hegel's and Mr. Hegel's stacks of papers encroached upon the teachers' worktable, lunching with my colleagues during third period became for me a much-anticipated ritual.

When the bell rang, ending second period, my students tore out of the room, and I gathered my things quickly while Miss Rigg's students entered. Miss Rigg was always delayed because she had to haul her supplies from class to class. She and her class were in the throes of an ongoing negotiation concerning their rights and privileges upon entering the room. They thought they should be allowed to enter as though entering a playground, and she thought they should enter as though entering a hotel lobby. Miss Rigg and her class were getting nowhere in the settlement of this dispute. The students came clamoring into the room, chasing one another up and down the aisles, sitting on the desktops, and conversing loudly and, at times, obscenely. One student might throw open the window if he felt warm, and another would fuss about being cold. The best-behaved kids settled into a chair with a snack and a messaging device. The peripatetic Miss Rigg soon wheeled her cart into the room and, seeing the disorder, exploded, scolding in a voice so loud the birds on the trees outside scattered. This reprimand had the desired effect after a few repetitions, and the lesson at last commenced. I didn't get involved, since I was on my way out and they weren't my students. As long as they didn't destroy anything, I kept quiet. Besides, I had given Miss Rigg instructions on how much of the chalkboard she was allowed to use and where she might store a few of her things. I wasn't sure she was satisfied with her allocations, so I kept my conversations with her brief, lest she start negotiating with me for additional space. I arranged my lunch in my briefcase and fled, muttering a perfunctory good morning as I passed the usually frazzled Miss Rigg. She was too busy dressing down her students to answer. Luckily, she was young and pretty—a petite blonde—which served her well, since her clothing and her youthful shape assured her some attention when she started her class.

I always arrived for lunch in the office first. Then Wood arrived with his brown bag holding all the treasures of the deli. Finally, if she weren't busy, Worthington made an entrance, often with a gaggle of helpers in her wake, students from the various activities she sponsored—invariably young ladies with lofty ambitions, like herself.

Wood and I had been doing our clandestine surveillance of my desk during this period for a couple of weeks, but we could only tape every other day since we used the camera as a monitor to view the tape on alternate days. After taping on the previous day, I brought the camera to lunch and positioned it on the table so we both could watch the little screen. We played the tape in fast-forward, looking for a malefactor. It only took a few minutes. So far we had not seen anything suspicious, though the thief, in spite of our efforts, had glommed a nice pen (which I had found and thought was a real gem) and a pad of Post-it Notes (which are surprisingly expensive). We decided either the crook had struck on a day when we were using the camera to view a tape, or he was a very clever thief indeed. Perhaps, Wood surmised, he waited patiently in an inconspicuous spot during my preparation period—sixth period—until I would leave the room to go on an errand or to the bathroom, and then he slipped into my empty room to do his mischief. Wood encouraged me to be scrupulous about locking my door whenever I left, and especially overnight, if I expected the third period surveillance to bear fruit. I wondered what kind of strange child would waste a period casing my room, waiting for an opportunity to grab a pad of Post-it Notes; but then, it wasn't the notes he wanted to get, it was my goat. And he was succeeding.

Mrs. Worthington eyed us suspiciously while we watched the tapes, keeping aloof. She allowed the surveillance might discover the wrongdoer, but she suspected we were peeping at the lovely Miss Rigg, a suspicion that we reinforced by chuckling from time to time, and which Mr. Wood confirmed for Mrs. Worthington by exclaiming, "Damn, girl" at one point, then excusing himself while Worthington rolled her eyes.

A student named Kim often trailed Mrs. Worthington into the office and joined us for a while. She was the captain of Worthington's Ushers Club, a group of conscientious students, whose task it was to coordinate assembly programs and special occasions, like Women's Day or Career Day. They also conducted tours for visitors—requiring the Ushers to be a well-groomed, mannerly crew—and they were generally available for any kind of occasion when the school needed a student-emissary and wanted to avoid embarrassment. Kim did not disappoint. She dressed and coiffed herself mindfully, sometimes wearing a pinstriped suit like her mentor, Worthington. Her hair had a flip and a part, and sometimes a little bow. She was not afraid to speak and had the confidence to speak to adults.

"Oh, Mrs. Worthington, I'm so busy, I'll never get home tonight," said Kim one morning from the door of the office. She could move no closer since Mrs. Hegel was storing a television on a cart near her other cart, negating all available sitting room beyond the spots taken by my cohorts and me.

Worthington, opening her Tupperware, addressed Kim as a peer, "What's on for this afternoon, Kim?"

"What's not? I have to finish the database showing which speaker will be in which room. I still have to contact some of the presenters and confirm that they will show up. I want to format that database into a kind of brochure or program that we can distribute...."

"A program? Do you know how to do that?" asked Worthington. "Because I don't."

"Never fear, chief, I'm on it." Reaching into her attaché case, Kim fingered the manila folders she used to organize her projects, and she found the prototype of her proposed brochure. She extended it to Wood, whom she could reach by twisting around the TV on the cart, and he passed it on to Worthington. The document was neat and tidy with columns and rows showing speakers, rooms, and times. And it was embellished with tasteful splashes of clip art—a pen here and a mortarboard there—making it a very professional-looking document.

"How'd you do that?" asked Wood.

"Magic," said Kim. "InDesign. Desktop publishing software. We use it to lay out the newspaper..."

"Can I get a copy of that software?" asked Wood.

"Not legally," said Kim, "but I'll see what I can do. Come up to Mrs. Worthington's office after school and bring a blank CD. That's where I'll be making this document spiffy."

"OK," said Wood, unwrapping a sandwich. I determined it to be either chicken salad or tuna salad, so I set about sniffing to determine which. Whatever it was, it was stuffed into one of the largest Kaiser rolls I'd ever seen. This roll was as big as a newsboy's cap.

Worthington reclaimed Kim's attention. "How late will you be staying in school?"

"Till around five, I guess...then I'll be up all night, I guess, studying for Anatomy."

"All right, but I have an appointment after school and I can't join you. Could you lock my office when you finish?" Worthington passed the document back toward Kim.

"No problemo," said Kim. "I'll use my key. Are you and the hubby having dinner out?"

"I wish," said Worthington. "No, I have to attend a meeting and pick up some materials for the next round of benchmark tests." Worthington was also the testing coordinator for our school, a position that required more and more of her time since the No Child Left Behind laws made testing the activity of primary importance in schools.

We heard a commotion in the hallway. A student was telling another student he'd meet him soon in the bathroom, and he was not modulating his voice; if anything, he had raised the volume of his voice to an obstreperous level in defiance of the classes in session throughout the hallway. Unfortunately for us, this youth slouched into our space and sidled past Kim, leering at her with wistful eyes and murmuring, "'Sup?" He took no pains to avoid contact with her body in the constricted space, and Kim showed no distress at this, but returned, "Hi, Gus."

Seeing Mrs. Worthington, Gus instinctively hiked up his pants, which were drooping below his buttocks in the back, revealing boxers that were printed in a Campbell tartan. He failed, however, to adjust his pants to Mrs. Worthington's satisfaction.

"Augustus Merriwether," Worthington interrupted Augustus's gaze at Kim. She pointed at his colorful drawers with disapprobation. "What are you doing here?"

"I *had* to come here," sighed Gus, hitching his pants again as his eyes rolled toward the ceiling.

"Why?"

"Miss Rigg threw me out of class," Augustus complained. "Told me to sit in here." He stretched forth a note with one hand while he used his other hand to hold up his pants by grasping them near the crotch. Kim took the opportunity to withdraw, saying, "Bye, Mrs. Worthington. I'll have the program for you tomorrow," and she squeezed past Gus, who did not give her an inch and kissed the breeze in her wake as he held the crotch of his pants tighter.

"Well you can't stay in here," said Worthington, "There's no room. What exactly did you do to make Miss Rigg ask you to leave?"

"Nothin'! She's crazy! She says I called her a bitch, but I was talking to myself."

"Take your hands off your crotch and pull up your pants," Worthington ordered. "I can see your underwear."

"That's not my *underwear*. I have two pairs of boxers on, just so you *can't* see my underwear."

Wood and I chuckled at this, but Worthington did not see the humor. "It says on this note that you refused to stop listening to your iPod and that you called Miss Rigg a 'b.' Is that right?"

"I don't even have an iPod. Oh, my *God!* Check my pockets." Gus extended his arms. "And I didn't call her anything. She doesn't like me. She always says I'm doin' somethin' or sayin' somethin'. She's crazy. I don't know why y'all hire crazy people—"

Worthington stiffened. "Pull up those pants, or I'll pull them up for you—and I'll pull them up to your neck. Here, take this sheet of paper and your note and go to the library. I want you to write two hundred and fifty words explaining exactly what happened in Miss Rigg's room, and bring it back to me by the end of this period. And you better return it by the end of the period, or you will answer to me."

I noticed on the face of Augustus, as he hiked up his britches and took the papers from Worthington, the distinctive trace of the smile that forms on the countenance of a youth who has gotten away with something. Weighing his behavior against the consequences he'd received, his deal was not so bad. He'd get a free trip to the bathroom to meet so-and-so; he'd miss a class; he'd dash off an explanation of fifty words or so for Worthington; and all would be well. I felt sure Miss Rigg would be happy with a period free of Augustus also, so it was a win-win. Heaving a sigh of mock indignation, Augustus took the blank paper and withdrew.

"These kids," said Worthington.

"I had Augustus in the tenth grade," said Wood. "He seemed to have a checklist of misbehaviors he had to complete every day. Late to class—check. Unprepared—check. Insult the teacher's clothes—check. He had his own agenda. Yet, I remember he was into *Julius Caesar* and understood completely the idea that idealism is dangerous."

"You remember that?" I asked. I wondered where in *Julius Caesar* the idea that idealism is dangerous came in. Wasn't it the story of a group of bumbling idiots who struggle for power with a rising despot? Yet, the concept that idealism is dangerous did sound appealing and I promised myself I'd look into it the next time I went through the play.

"What do you plan to do with Kim's software?" I asked Wood, whose lunch I determined to be chicken salad. He was clearly enjoying the size of his sandwich, which had the circumference of a small pizza. He was washing it down with a sixteen-ounce Coke, a beverage I had not touched in sixteen years and that I missed as much as I missed the cigarettes of my youth.

"I don't know. It depends on how well I can make copies of that software. I wouldn't mind having classes create newspapers or brochures."

I thought, *Damn, Wood. That'll take hours to learn; it'll be hell to teach, impossible to grade, and is just plain risky. Don't you have enough to do just keeping up with the normal stuff?* But I said, "Good idea. Keep me posted on how that works out."

Wood surprised us then by launching into another story about his previous teaching assignment. This time it was about starving students. I wondered, as the story proceeded, if Augustus, or Kim, or both had motivated the telling of the tale, or whether it was the size of his sandwich, or the prospect of teaching something entirely new. *Something* provoked the telling.

He began, as he would begin all of his stories, by stating that the events took place in Peale High School, and he related his tale, as usual, with perfect solemnity. I think he showed less animation the more preposterous the events. He didn't flinch once, as he hadn't when he had told us the tale of the room wired for electric shocks, nor did he show any sign that he might be exaggerating.

I'll do my best to relate what I heard. I had not yet conceived the idea of taping Wood when he told a story, so I may have missed a detail or two. Wood explained that the students back at Peale succumbed to a "fad of fasting" that got out of control. The trend of not eating caught on like any teenage trend, like an epidemic. They refused to eat—in school and at home—and they became terribly malnourished and emaciated. The poor students sat in their chairs in a daze, unable to concentrate, hardly able to lift a pencil. More and more students joined in this debilitating trend, which precluded any learning, until the administration of the school decided they must do something. So the administration published an edict saying that teachers should no longer teach the subjects they'd been teaching, but instead they should prepare meals for students—in class—and make these meals irresistible. The thinking was that once students began eating again, they would fatten up and regain the power to concentrate, and then they could go back to their regular lessons. Moreover, the administration decided that the fare that would do the trick was French food, since that cuisine has such a renowned reputation.

So the school's administration decreed that students should take three days off— these days were called Staff Development Days—during which some of the finest French chefs in the city would come to the school and give the teachers a crash course in

French cooking, and the teachers would turn around and create irresistible meals for their students. And, said Wood, the teachers in the school emerged as pretty good chefs. On the day students returned to school, a contingent of teachers prepared a sumptuous French meal in the cafeteria, while the rest of the staff prepared their rooms as dining rooms, replete with decorations that evinced a French ambiance—posters of the Loire Valley, wine labels, and ads for Quimper adorned the bulletin boards. For lunch, there was a mousse of foie gras with truffles, duck breast in orange sauce, a roasted endive salad, and some potatoes mashed with garlic and oil. For dessert, teachers offered a rich vanilla custard tart with whipped cream and caramelized fruit. But though the teachers prepared the meals well and presented them well, the students refused to eat. The teachers heard a few "yucks," a few orange slices flew through the air, but mainly the skinny students sat at their tables and stared into space. However, Wood emphasized, there were a few kids who ate robustly and proclaimed that this was the best meal ever.

The administration of Peale served French food for two weeks, but the students would not eat, except for those few who adored the food. So the administration, thinking the reason for the menu's rejection lay in its culinary sophistication, decided to stick with the plan of preparing meals for students but opted this time to prepare basic American food. Once again the administration required Staff Development Days, though teachers only needed two days this time since they had picked up so much skill during their last lessons. And when the students returned this time, the dining rooms looked like good old American diners and the menu consisted of chicken with rice, smothered in gravy, with some buttered string beans on the side, and a big gooey brownie for dessert. But the same thing happened. Most of the students did not touch their lunches, while that same group of students, who enjoyed the French cuisine and were getting a little fat, loved it. The gourmand-students were reaching over when they finished their plates and finishing off the leavings of their fellow students, who were wasting away.

After a few weeks of American food, the fasting students were getting dangerously thin. They could hardly walk down the corridors. One might see them sitting on the floor in the hallways, their heavy heads tilted onto one another's shoulders.

The school's administration soon abandoned the American menu and called for some new Staff Development Days. Appalled by all this staff development, the teachers union protested, saying the administration was illegally asking teachers to teach subjects outside their areas of certification, but no one paid any attention to this. The school decided to train teachers in the art of cooking soul food. This, they said, was bound to work.

Chefs got the teachers up to speed in a day. The new menu consisted of a potluck gumbo with chunks of ham and shrimp. There were fluffy grits and sweet potato pie. But everything went untouched, even the dessert, which was a carrot cake with cream cheese frosting, the kind of dessert that would break the diet of the most disciplined diabetic. But the only diners were the usual diners, who ate the meals with gusto and proclaimed them the finest meals of all, but these satisfied customers were few and far between.

The administration had run out of ideas. Students still came to school, but they were like victims of a concentration camp, all atremble, parched of lips, their skin dry and lifeless, their bellies distended. They were like paper-thin sacks of protruding bones.

Wood told us how he was down in the principal's office when the problem reached a crisis. An emaciated kid staggered into the principal's office and fell into one of the principal's guest chairs. His frightened teacher had sent him to the office, accompanied by one of the gourmand-students, after he had collapsed and fallen from his classroom dining table. Held up by his chubby fellow student, he managed to get to the principal's office and sit in a chair that faced the principal. But soon he collapsed from the chair and fell onto the floor without a sound. The principal rushed to his side and, kneeling, propped the limp student's weary head onto his knee. Secretaries came from behind their desks, and other staff members filed into the office, along with Wood and the food-loving student, and they all stood around the pathetic scene of the principal supporting the skeletal head of the fasting student.

The principal shed a tear of desperation. "Why is this, son, why?" asked the principal, "Why do you all refuse to eat?"

And the boy, who looked like Death, and whose breath came in shallow gasps, turned his skull slowly toward the principal and whispered, "Because we aren't hungry. That's why we don't eat."

And the last flicker of life left the poor boy's eyes...

When Wood finished the story, Worthington and I looked at each other, speechless again. He finished his story and his enormous sandwich simultaneously and, as he took a last swig of Coke, he said, "No lie."

Worthington, her eyebrows furrowed, turned to Wood and was about to ask a question when Augustus breezed in with his essay. He still held up his sagging pants by clutching them at the crotch. He now sported white earbud headphones with wires that extended deep into his pants pocket. At the sides of his lips were traces of a cheese-flavored snack. And the essay he held was so ragged it looked as though Ptolemy wrote it and rolled into a scroll a few thousand years ago. Augustus stretched the scroll to Worthington, who accepted it gingerly and unrolled it.

"What is this?" she asked.

Wood and I began to chuckle, which infected Augustus. He said, amused, "That's a good essay. It shows how crazy that woman is. How she picks on me while everyone else is doing the same thing.... She's a racist. She told me I don't belong in this school. She told my mom I should be in a vocational school...."

"Take those headphones off and put them away," said Worthington, looking at the essay, "or I'll take the iPod."

"But it's not *on*. I'm not *listening* to anything."

Wood and I cracked up, since we could hear the muffled bass coming from the phones.

Worthington glared at Gus, and he took the earbuds out of his ears with his customary sigh of righteous indignation. "Are you going to give that essay to Miss Rigg?" he asked. "I need the credit."

"No," said Worthington, "there is some interesting graffiti on this that Mr. Squires might be interested in."

"I didn't *do* that," said Gus, "Oh, my *God!*"

Wood and I chuckled. The bell rang. And Gus ran away.

5. Chaucer, Napoleon, testing, and surveillance

DURING Christmas break I conceived the idea of transcribing Mr. Wood's stories into a book. I recall lounging on the couch one afternoon, imbibing an after-lunch martini (I always started early during vacations—what were vacations for?). And as the TV droned meaninglessly in the background, and Mrs. Kessler was involved somewhere in the house doing three or four things at once, I began thinking about the desolate stretches of free time I would have in a few years when I retired. And then I had an epiphany! If I collected a bunch of Wood's stories, I could work on them during retirement, and turn them into a book or something. I needed to do something, or I was afraid I'd start drinking and watching TV after breakfast. I always fancied the idea of becoming an author; I just didn't have anything to write. I assumed he had more stories, and they needed to be published—they were very entertaining—and if I collected a number of them, they'd fill a pretty good book and give me something to do. I'd be a writer.

The idea that I might be appropriating someone's intellectual property never entered my thoughts. Though I resolved to save the actual drafting of Wood's tales for when I retired, I spent the rest of my vacation working on notes and outlines for the two stories that Wood had already told—the one about the disciplinary machine and the one about the starving students. I didn't want to forget the details of these stories, and I was pleased with how working on these notes occupied my free time.

During the very first week of the new year, my class and I were reading the General Prologue to *The Canterbury Tales* and I came across the following words spoken by the narrator:

> For certainly, as you all know so well,
> He who repeats a tale after a man
> Is bound to say, as nearly as he can,
> Each single word, if he remembers it,
> However rudely spoken or unfit,
> Or else the tale he tells will be untrue,
> The things pretended and the phrases new.

And I thought to myself that it would be a good idea to tell Wood's stories exactly as he said them instead of paraphrasing, and I resolved to retell Wood's tales with all the details of the original, just as Chaucer's narrator recommended. I found among my possessions a small tape recorder that used mini-tapes, like the kind used in a telephone answering machine, and I resolved the next time Wood told one of his tall tales, I would save it verbatim.

On the day before the citywide benchmark tests were to commence at Northwest, Mrs. Worthington wheeled her cart, loaded like a pack mule, full of testing materials, into the crowded English office, and her protégé Kim was right behind her, jabbering about a meeting of something called the "ASA." Kim again was forced to stop at the door and peer over the cart to talk to her mentor. "Can't we use your room for our meeting, please...please...please?" pleaded Kim.

"OK, but don't let anybody touch anything."

"Yes! I won't. Can you join us?"

"Kim, I can't talk to you right now. I've got to sort out all of these materials." Worthington was harried. She exhaled with resignation and let her shoulders droop.

"I can help you sort them out," said Kim, "I'll go get Lorraine. We'll finish in no time."

"That would be great, but it's illegal. Students aren't allowed near these materials." Worthington was reaching into the reserves of her patience. "Take Lorraine and go and make an agenda for the ASA. There's no room in here for another person anyway."

"What's the ASA?" asked Wood, handling a corned beef on rye. He had been on a Jewish deli kick lately, and he liked his sandwiches thick with meat and slathered with yellow mustard. He was scarfing this one down greedily. *Must be really good,* I thought. *Nicely marbled corned beef, very little gristle....* I caught a whiff of sesame seeds.

"Any cheese on that sandwich?" I asked, fantasizing Swiss.

"The Altruistic Students of America," said Kim.

"No cheese on corned beef...that's *traif.* You should know that," Wood joked.

"Go, Kim. Shoo!" said Worthington as she began to unpack her cart and sort the testing materials on the worktable, which wasn't easy since one of Mr. Hegel's students had created a panorama of the Battle of Waterloo that took up half the table. With Wood and his generous sandwich on one side of the table and me and my trivial lunch on the other, there was very little space for Worthington. The student's rendition of Waterloo consisted of two hills of green papier-mâché on a plywood base, and in the valley of the hills a pandemonium of soldiers, some dressed in red and some in blue, fought in a scrum. I suppose the student had bought these soldiers in a toy store, and they were certainly soldiers from the 19th century, but I'd have to leave it to Mr. Hegel to judge their authenticity. The soldiers were squeezed into a violent jumble, and the student had mangled some of the soldiers in an effort to show the brutality of the battle—to the extent that one poor Frenchman's head hung from a thread. On the top of each of the facing hills sat the generals. Wellington to my left, on his rearing horse, extending his sword upward to command an attack, and Napoleon, to my right, sitting on his mount quite dejected, his horse grazing on the green papier-mâché. The real genius of the rendition lay in how the student made Napoleon so small he seemed like a dwarf or a baby with a big head. Poor Napoleon's feet did not even reach their stirrups. Much to the student's credit, I thought, Napoleon's hand did rest inside his waistcoat. I don't know how the student rendered Napoleon so creatively; he must have taken a number of different toy soldiers and amalgamated them to achieve his effect. Unfortunately, this panorama left little room for lunch at the worktable.

"I declare," I said, "will Mr. Hegel turn this place into history's storage locker, or what?" There was a large replica of a cotton gin under the table at our feet.

Wood dropped a crumb or two of rye bread on the hills of Waterloo and brushed them away. "Testing again?"

As testing coordinator, Worthington took delivery of loads of testing materials from downtown; then she organized the operation and sent the finished materials back to the District for scoring. "Check your memo, Mr. Wood. You'll be administering the second benchmark test next Tuesday," she said.

"Good," I said. I liked when the school gave tests. It was a free period for me. All I had to do was give some instructions, start the test, and relax. What was wrong with that? I didn't even have to grade the damned thing.

"Tests make me sick," said Wood, voicing the usual but inexplicable feeling of most of the staff.

"Now, now," said Worthington, counting reams of tests and setting them on the table, careful not to interfere with the Battle of Waterloo.

"I like a nice test," I said. "Should we cover our bulletin boards with newspaper, as usual?"

"I'm afraid so," said Worthington, amused.

Covering the bulletin boards was a mandate designed to make sure students did not find any illicit information on the walls of the room during a test. I had no problem with this since I did not decorate my bulletin boards. But this business of covering the bulletin boards was a problem for some teachers and especially Wood since bulletin boards were one of his fortes. At one time I recall he'd fashioned a kind of board game called "The History of English Literature" on the bulletin board in the back of his room. Using different colored construction paper and collages cut from posters, he'd made a rendition of Chutes and Ladders showing a chronology of English Literature. Very nice, but I couldn't help thinking that the poor fellow needed to get a life. Now, during the test, he'd have to cover all of his stimulating artwork, poor sap. After all, who knows, the test might ask, "What was the color of Shakespeare's pants?" and a student could get the answer from looking at a picture of the Bard on the wall.

"That's it!" Wood swatted at an imaginary fly. "No more decorations on my bulletin boards! I've had it. Let me ask you something," Wood pointed the crust of his sandwich at me, "Have you noticed the difference between the scores that students get in the morning on these tests and the scores they get in the afternoon?

"Not really," I said. Where was he going with this, I wondered. Did he actually look at the scores?

"How do they differ?" asked Worthington.

"Scores climb as the day goes by."

"So you think students are comparing notes when they leave the room, and that they're sharing with their friends?" Worthington deduced.

"Do you think they're not? Are you aware of how much cheating goes on on these tests?"

"Enough to skew the results?" Worthington stopped counting for a moment.

"Perhaps your classes later in the day are smarter," I offered.

"Puh-lease," Wood said. "I know for a fact that kids take pictures of the test with their cell phones and send them along to others. I've seen them. Who knows? They may even communicate with cell phones during the test."

I realized my students could easily do this, since I kept myself very busy during these tests, catching up on paperwork, and I rarely watched the test-takers. But I said, incredulously, "They talk on the phone? While the test is going on?"

My colleagues looked at me as though I were a Martian. "Text," they said together.

"Ohhhh."

Worthington was listening to Wood's rant, though I wished he would shut up, since Worthington might discuss this problem with higher-ups and they, in turn, would concoct plans to thwart cheating, which might result in more work for me—like having to walk around during the test or collect every cell phone.... Case in point: the cover-the-bulletin-board rule.

"I caught one kid with all the answers on a strip of paper before he took the test. Now how did that happen?" said Wood.

"Did you report it?" asked Worthington.

"Yes, but Mrs. Hegel told me simply to destroy his answer sheet so his test wouldn't count in the statistics. Let me ask you this," Wood was aiming his crust at Mrs. Worthington now. "What are these tests supposed to reveal? I mean, when we get the results."

"They are supposed to show which teachers are doing a good job and which are not."

"Right, OK, so here's the thing that gets me: When I look at the results, on that printout we get that shows all the teachers in the department and the average score of all their classes, I have noticed that the class averages for every teacher are almost identical.... Look, we all teach the tenth grade. Mr. Kessler, what was the average score for your tenth graders on the last benchmark?"

"Around eighty-seven percent," I said.

"And you, Mrs. Worthington, what were your scores?"

"About the same."

"And so were mine. Eighty-eight point six, if I remember correctly," said Wood. "And all the other teachers of the tenth grade had the same. Now, here's the thing: How can these tests distinguish things like who is doing the right thing and who is not if there is no difference in the results? Suppose the administration decides to distribute merit pay based on the results of this test. Will I get merit pay by scoring one percentage point above Mr. Kessler?"

We saw where Wood was going and we laughed, but it was the laugh of those who understand the absurdity of a situation but also know that resistance is futile since the situation is imposed by a higher power. "Scores will increase dramatically if they institute merit pay," I joked, "because we all will cheat. I know I will."

"And ignore those cell phones," said Worthington, who had resumed her collation of tests.

I was hoping Wood would tell another story, perhaps on the subject of testing, from his days at Peale, and I had my tape recorder ready, but when he finished his sandwich, he said, "Time to check the latest surveillance."

"Oh, good," I said. I had the video camera in my briefcase next to the mini tape recorder. I found watching these tapes rather tedious by this time. Essentially, they showed a picture of my desk and its environs, including Miss Rigg and her cart and a few students in the front row. Though we played the tape in fast-forward to save time, I was getting sick of seeing nothing but Miss Rigg moving herky-jerky back and forth, and a few students in the front row who never stopped chattering, and my desk, which was embarrassingly neat. While Worthington busied herself with the testing materials, we zoomed through the surveillance tape. And this time we found something interesting.

Miss Rigg was about to distribute a worksheet of some kind, and she was explaining directions. Sitting near Rigg's desk, as usual, was a blond girl, who wore a leather jacket and had a ring through her lip, chattering non-stop with a lanky dark-skinned youth who sat next to her. Same old thing. But then, as Miss Rigg finished giving out the papers (though Blondie did not finish chattering), someone in the back of the room got Rigg's attention, and she went over to my desk (stopping to get Blondie started) and took my stapler. Then she disappeared from the frame for a while, and when she returned, she did not put the stapler back on my desk but, instead, held it while she gave some additional instructions and, finally, she put the stapler on her cart.

"Miss Rigg took my stapler!" I said. "It was missing yesterday, and then it turned up on the bookcase in the back of the room today."

"Ah-ha," said Wood. He continued the fast-forward to the end of the class, and we could clearly see the stapler on Miss Rigg's cart as she left the room.

"Do you think Rigg has been responsible for all the misplaced items—and the theft?" asked Wood. Worthington shook her head.

"Yes," I said, "She's a nut. She never says hello to me when she comes into the room. And she screams so loud she could wake the dead. Have you ever noticed that she lets the copy machine run while she goes somewhere; then she makes a million copies and forgets to retrieve them? Sometimes they sit in here for days."

Just then, as though led by the cunning hand of Chance, Rigg walked into the office. We all looked up, suddenly quiet. People know you are talking about them when you get so suddenly quiet, and Rigg looked at us suspiciously. "I forgot to pick up my copies," she said. She reached into the exit tray of the copy machine and pulled out a big stack of papers. "What?" she asked in response to the pregnant silence.

"Good morning, Miss Rigg," I said. She smiled absently and hurried off. Her class was waiting.

When she was out of earshot, I exclaimed, "Rigg took my stapler, and my teachers' edition, and my jar of candies, and my umbrella—my *umbrella!* She's been helping herself to the items in my drawer! She's crazy as a loon. Remember how she thought school started the week before it did? How about the time she forgot she had a class until a student came in here and reminded her? She's nuts."

"So Gus was right?" said Wood.

"Gus? About what?" I asked.

"That she's crazy."

"She's just new," said Worthington.

"New, my ass," I said. "She's a crook!"

6. Accusations, observations, obscure language, and Kay

THE next day I confronted Miss Rigg with the issue of the misplaced stapler, and she apologized, saying that she had taken it from the room and hadn't realized it. I then asked her about the teachers' edition of my textbook, and she said she had indeed left it in the back of the classroom after using it to look something up. She was unsure about the board erasers.

I questioned Miss Rigg about these items as soon as she had wheeled her cart into the room and was about to initiate her usual routine of screaming her unruly class into submission. Because I'd interrupted Miss Rigg's opening remarks and engaged her in conversation, her students went unchecked and continued their playground antics. Gus, who came in a bit late, took a seat on the windowsill in the back of the room and began to amuse a small group of listeners with a story. Blondie got busy pecking at her cell phone and blabbing simultaneously with her neighbor. There were a couple of students who lined up near Miss Rigg and me, wanting to ask her a question. Another student had her hand raised, wanting to go to the bathroom. And another girl was pulling on a boy's jacket asking for something to be returned to her. The general din grew louder as I discussed matters with Miss Rigg, who cast an agitated glance at her class while I spoke.

"I found my pointer behind the file cabinet one day," I said, arranging my lunch in my briefcase.

"I must have put it there to get it out of the way," said Rigg. She scowled ineffectually at her class. The girl who wanted something returned said, "Miss Rigg, Jorge has my highlighter and won't give it back."

"I keep finding things misplaced," I said.

Gus's group laughed uproariously at Gus's pantomiming giving someone the finger.

"I'll pay more attention," she said, trying to evade me and get her class started. "Could I—"

"And then there's the matter of the things missing from my desk," I said. I pointed the banana I was about to put in my briefcase at her.

"What's that?" Miss Rigg ceased apologizing and assumed a puzzled expression. Although the class's noise had geared up a notch and Miss Rigg needed to do something about this, she suddenly seemed intent on what I had to say.

"There are items missing from my desk," I said, "Pens, batteries, paper clips, a screwdriver... Do you know anything about a flash dr—?"

"Why are you saying this?" she asked, reddening. "What are you saying?"

"I've lost a lot of things," I said.

"Are you accusing me of—stealing?" Miss Rigg forgot all about her class, half of whom were out of their seats and paying visits to the other half. Gus was attempting a planche on the windowsill.

I spoke over the noise, "We've done surveillance on your room and—"

"Surveillance!" echoed Miss Rigg. She glanced at the spot where the camera had stood those many days. She cocked her head in disbelief, "Surveillance?"

"Yes," I said. "That video camera I kept over there has been on all this time...."

Miss Rigg smiled vaguely as it sank in, "You spied on me?"

"Well not exactly on you—"

I was about to explain the whole process, but Miss Rigg lost her cool. Her class was veering out of control, but she aimed her invective at me, "You think I stole your stuff?" she asked, stepping toward me with her chest puffed up and her eyes widening.

I withdrew, clutching my banana.

"I never touched your desk!" exclaimed Rigg, "What would I

want with a screwdriver? I have never so much as even opened one of your drawers." Her color deepened. "Paper clips, huh? So you're worried about missing paper clips? I don't know what's in your drawers, and I don't care what's in your drawers. Whatta ya have in there, anyway, a year's supply of bananas? A million apples? Yeah, I want to steal your bananas." She made as if to snatch the banana from my hand, and we fumbled with it. "That's right! I'm gonna steal your fruit! I'll tell you what: Let's see if we can make your desk a little less tempting—" And she strode over to my desk and, with a swoop of her arm, pushed everything onto the floor. This brought the students, who had grown increasingly quiet during Rigg's mounting anger, to attention. They settled into their seats and stared. The line of supplicants in the front of the room hurried back to their places.

"Miss Rigg..." I said.

She turned toward me, holding my pointer—which she had spared from the dumping—in her fist. "Now get out," she said. "I don't know anything about your goddamn batteries. And I didn't take your stuff. Now *piss off!*" She pointed toward the door with my pointer.

My impression was that the class wanted to see my response—they stared at me, rapt—but the look on Miss Rigg's face brooked no further discussion. Fumbling with my briefcase, I left for the English office, though I dropped my apple on the way, to the utter delight of the class. The laughter of Gus was quite distinguishable; "Oh my *God!*" he said as I fled, "That's fucked *up!*"

As I was leaving, Miss Rigg redirected her anger toward her class. "As for you," she remonstrated, still in possession of the pointer, "you listen to me! I'm sick of coming into this room and being treated like a dummy! You're taking advantage of me, and I'm not going to tolerate it anymore...." I could still hear her reading the riot act to her class as I crossed the hall into the English office.

I said nothing about this incident when I arrived for lunch. Wood sat alone, absorbed in a cheesesteak from the truck down the street and a document that I recognized all too well. I was a little shaken by the incident with Miss Rigg, but the document before Mr. Wood filled me with dread of another caliber. It was an Observation form. An assistant principal had observed Mr. Wood's class and rated his performance. This meant she would soon observe a class of mine, and there was no school routine I dreaded more than the Observation.

"Were you observed?" I asked, sitting and examining the terrible bruise on my apple.

"Yes."

"Anything interesting?"

Wood looked up, perplexed. "I was observed by the new assistant principal—"

"Frau Schlect," I interjected, giving the "r" and the second "c" the best uvular rolls I could.

"Yes. Schlect sat in the back of my room—she has very nice legs, don't you think?—and she scribbled and she scribbled on her clipboard while the class and I discussed an essay topic on *The Metamorphosis*."

"She wears interesting shoes," I said. Ms. Schlect's shoes terrified me. Her heels were sometimes three inches tall or more, and I could hear her clicking down the hallways. Sometimes I imagined she was coming toward my room if I heard a *click click click* in the hallway—even if it wasn't her—which caused my heart to skip a beat. Soon she'd be clicking her way into my room, clipboard in hand, ready to observe—with her hot-shot teaching ideas, and her something-to-prove attitude. I had had an understanding with her predecessor: I was an old, tenured teacher from another era, and what I did in class was tolerable because old dogs don't learn new tricks and the students were in acceptable order. But now—oy!

"Yes, nice shoes," said Wood. "Anyhow, she has written a comment on my Observation that I don't quite understand. Maybe you can understand it." He handed me the form and pointed to the comment.

It read: *Your rubric does not reflect differentiated instruction and, therefore, a criterion-referenced test will not provide disaggregated data.*

"Now what do you suppose that means?" asked Wood.

I was perusing the rest of the form, hoping to find some damning criticism, but I couldn't find any, and Wood was rated as "satisfactory," which is the best rating the form allows. "I don't know," I said. "I think I know what a 'rubric' is. Isn't it one of those matrices where you show your students how to get a good grade?"

"Something like that. But I wonder how the rubric can 'reflect differentiated instruction'? That's a good one."

"Worthington would know. Let's ask Worthington when she comes in. She's been to college more recently than we have."

"Good idea. By the way, I have some bad news about our surveillance."

"What?"

"We've been found out, discovered; we'll have to abort the mission."

Wood must have watched the most recent tape on his own. He had been using his camera with his class, and I'd been giving it to him as soon as my surveillances were done. "Oh, no." I said, though I had already aborted the mission—around the time the contents of my desk hit the floor. Still, I was dying to know what Wood had seen. Worthington arrived just then, though, and the conversation shifted. She had had a short, impromptu meeting outside the door, where we could not see with whom she spoke, something about balances and accounts, and then she came into the room looking professional, as usual, in broad pinstripes and high heels. I did not find Worthington's heels nearly as threatening as Frau Schlect's, though I'd mistaken Worthington's clicking down the hall for Schlect's on occasion and was frightened by false fire. Worthington sat and fished her Tupperware out of her big bag.

"Have you been observed?" asked Wood.

"Not yet," said Worthington.

"Mr. Kessler and I have been trying to figure out what Ms. Schlect meant by this comment on my Observation," Wood handed the document to Worthington.

"How did the Observation go?" asked Worthington.

"Not bad. Schlect and I get along."

Worthington read the obscure passage and responded, "That Schlect is a piece of work. I've had meetings with her. She has some strange ideas. She's the one who is pushing to break the school into small learning communities."

"Oh, no," Wood and I said in unison.

"Oh, yes," said Worthington. "As far as I can see, what she is saying here is that you needed more than one grading criteria for your lesson to accommodate the various students in the class."

"But I don't have various students. That's what she means

by 'differentiation,' I know, but the students in this school are tracked, so they're not different," said Wood.

"Even so, she probably thinks you should differentiate instruction for multiple intelligence."

"I don't think there is such a thing as multiple intelligence," said Wood. "You know there's no real research on the subject. It's just someone's opinion."

I thought to myself, *'Differentiate instruction for multiple intelligence'? Worthington would make a good assistant principal herself with that kind of abstruse lingo.* I had no idea what these two were talking about at this point. I mumbled, "...multiple intelligence" to appear to be following the conversation, but my mind wandered to thinking about strategies I might adopt to address the problem of my imminent Observation. If Ms. Schlect came into my class unannounced and saw what I was actually doing, she'd be very unhappy. Like Wood, I was reading *The Metamorphosis* with my class, but in a way that someone like Schlect would deplore. The class was reading by turns, stopping periodically to have a discussion. Schlect would hate that—it would be much too pedestrian and dull for her. So what was I to do? There were times in the past when I'd kept a handy, foolproof lesson in my top drawer, a fancy lesson I'd taken from a magazine article, which I knew would work, and I could whip it out when my observer showed up, and that would get me by. My tried and true lesson, however, was an analysis of "Trees" by Joyce Kilmer—*I think that I shall never see/a poem lovely as a tree*— and I couldn't figure out how to make a connection between this mock lesson, which had so often saved my bacon, and what I was actually doing at the present time. My students might wonder why we were suddenly, in the middle of *The Metamorphosis*, reading "Trees." What could Kilmer possibly have in common with Kafka? Some wise-guy student would probably say something right in front of Schlect, something like, "Uh, Mr. Kessler, what has this tree-thing got to do with the guy who turns into a bug?" And this made the ringer-lesson risky. A long grammar lesson was out, also. Ms. Schlect would pan a grammar lesson that lasted a whole period—too mechanical, none of those so-called critical thinking skills. Then I lit on an idea. Later in the day, I would sneak over to Wood's room and see what he was doing. Then I could replicate his lesson in my class. I'd just have to do a bit more snooping.

"You said you had some difficulty with your surveillance," I said, interrupting Wood's and Worthington's discussion about his Observation. Wood had just said, "Why would we teach three or four different lessons to one class, when the school could just track the students into three or four different tracks and give each one the same lesson?" I'm sure they didn't mind my interruption.

"What happened?" asked Worthington, amused, referring to our surveillance, which she had often criticized.

"We were found out. Made. We'll just have to accept that that we could not find solid evidence about who is the thief with our surveillance," said Wood.

"How were you discovered?" asked Worthington. She liked this.

"Rigg is really nutty," I said. They looked at me. "I'm just saying."

"Well," said Wood to me, "We had that camera pointed at your desk yesterday, and one of Miss Rigg's students, our old friend Gus..."

"Gus!" I repeated. "Goddamn Gus."

"Yes, Gus. He noticed the camera was on while he was returning from a walk to the trashcan. You can see him on the tape discovering that the camera is recording. He looks in the lens and says, 'Oh, shit, this thing is on.' Then he bends down, and he puts his face right up to the lens, and he flips us the bird. Then he stands up and starts to unzip his pants as though he's going to show his privates. The class is in hysterics while he tugs, very theatrically, on his zipper, but Miss Rigg intervenes at this point and orders him back to his seat.... Want to see the tape? It's pretty funny."

"No, thanks," said Worthington.

I said I'd like to see it. Gus was having too much fun. I decided he must be the thief... Hadn't Worthington said that the person you think is the crook probably is the crook? Wood handed the video camera to me and I prepared to watch the playback.

"So what does the rest of this thing mean, this..." Wood looked back at his Observation, "...*a criterion-referenced test will not provide disaggregated data?*"

"That one's beyond me," said Worthington.

Then it became obvious that Wood was about to begin another story. "Back at Peale," he said. I was just beginning to watch the little playback screen on the video camera when Wood said this, and I thought, *Quick, Kessler, get your tape recorder.* But, since I did not want Wood to know that I was taping him, I needed to quit the video playback discreetly and prepare my tape recorder without anyone noticing. So I casually stopped the video and moved the camera aside. Unfortunately, when I reached around to my briefcase to get the audio recorder, I elbowed the video camera to the edge of the table where it teetered. Luckily, Wood stopped it from falling with a "Whoa!" that interrupted his story. He looked at me with gentle accusation and I shrugged. Worthington's hand was on her heart. Then Wood continued his story, and I managed to make a clandestine recording.

I should admit that I have made some changes to Wood's stories, cleaning up syntax, replacing words, changing what worked orally into what works in writing as I saw fit and, in this story, since I had a devil of a time with the French (which Wood seemed to speak fluently), I used the translators in Google to figure out what was going on. Then I elicited the aid of the nurse from Humphrey Junior High, who is Canadian, and I sent her the French parts in an email. She made some corrections, and...well, here goes—the story as Wood told it:

My oldest and best friend at Peale, Ms. Kay Fortunata, walked into her school building one morning expecting an ordinary day. At this time in her career she always carried a huge knitting bag full of needlepoint projects, and this bag had become her trademark. On this day, she walked with enthusiasm and resolve because she was young and strong, and she had an important meeting with the principal later in the day, as well as five periods of English to teach. "I'll make short shrift of that principal's meeting, regardless of its importance," she decided, "and I will have some time to finish my needlepoint."

When Ms. Fortunata entered the school building and passed an unfamiliar security person at the door, she was not surprised. She supposed the usual person must be absent. But, when Kay peeked into the assistant principal's office and noticed a strange man behind Vice Principal Price's desk, she felt a touch of concern. Mr. Price was never absent. She looked around to share this anomaly with someone, but Ms. Fortunata found to her surprise that she did not recognize a single person in the hallway. Every face was unfamiliar. "Whoa, what's going on?" she wondered, looking this way and that for someone she knew.

Kay marched to the main office, determined to find out why she was here and everybody else, including Vice Principal Price, was absent. Was she supposed to be somewhere else? Had she missed a directive? Incredibly, when Kay entered the main office, she saw that here also the usual staff was missing, and a crew of strangers had taken their places. "Uh oh!" Ms. Fortunata gasped as she watched the inexplicable office workers behaving as though they belonged there.

Then, Kay sensed another peculiarity in the office. Besides being staffed by strangers, there was a difference in the office's ambiance, an odd variation in the overall noise. At first she could not put her finger on the subtle difference in the noise, but it sounded chattier, higher pitched, and more confused than usual. She stared into the office for a while, listening to the peculiar noise and gazing at the bizarre office replacements, until an attractive young secretary with a distinctive yellow scarf about her neck, approached Kay and said, most familiarly, "Bonjour, Madame Fortunata, comment allez-vous?" though Kay did not recognize the young woman one bit.

"Huh?" Kay responded. Then she dropped her bag of needlepoint and lesson plans, which fell to the floor and spilled, because she realized what the difference was in the office: Everyone was speaking French.

Forgetting her bag, dazed, Kay retraced her steps to the building's entrance. She wanted to look outside and check whether she had come to the right place. On her way to the door, she established conclusively that all the people in the building were indeed strangers, and they were all—not just the office workers, but all—speaking French, a language she did not understand. Incredibly, everyone seemed to know Kay, and they greeted her cheerily with "Bonjour, Madame...bonjour." Even the students (whom she often accused of not knowing English) spoke French.

Kay went gaga when she peeked outside and saw that she was in the right place. The old familiar neighborhood was still there, just as it had always been. Yet, behind her, within the school, she could plainly hear the babbling sound of français flowing freely down the corridors. "I must have had some kind of amnesia..." she said to herself, gazing at the familiar neighborhood. "...I must have missed a few days, or years... Maybe I should go home..."

Poor Kay. Certain realities now crowded around her. It occurred to her that if she had lost some time, she would have missed the important meeting she was scheduled to have with the principal and she would have a pile of work to catch up on. Kay looked at her watch, and it showed that there were no missing days. Her meeting with the principal was today, during her preparation period, after her first class. "But wait," she thought. "How shall I proceed if the meeting is in French?" Her knees felt suddenly weak. This meeting involved her lifelong dream to become a program coordinator and be in charge of her own program.

"Well, the show must go on, I guess," Kay said out loud, in English. She straightened herself, drew a deep breath, and turned back toward the weird school. She would just have to fake the lessons for her students and meet with the principal, who would more than likely be a foreigner. She retrieved her knitting bag and, mumbling bonjours to her new friends, started upstairs knowing that there would be no time for needlepoint today.

Kay had no problem teaching her classes. She gave the same lesson to each class. She delivered a lecture (in English) on the subject of dramatic irony in Oedipus Rex, and the class listened attentively, or as attentively as usual. At the conclusion of her lecture, she charged her students to find all the examples of dramatic irony they could find in the first part of the play. At first, the class looked puzzled—perhaps a little more than usual—and there was an awkward moment of silence and some obscure mumbling. However, after the students discussed this notion of "ironie" among themselves (in French), they shrugged their shoulders, laughed a Gallic laugh, and got to work. Kay answered a few questions from the stragglers and, although the teacher spoke in English and the students spoke in French, there were surprisingly few difficulties. In no time, all the students were wagging their little pens, writing their lists of examples. Although wearied by her effort to teach foreign students, Kay felt, for the moment, quite fortunate.

Soon, however, Kay began to dread her impending audience with the principal. Who would he be? A stranger, of course, and of course he would speak French. Could she ask him to speak English? Not a chance. What would the principal think of a

teacher who couldn't speak the native language? He would think
she were incompetent. Should she cancel? No, a teacher does
not cancel a meeting with a principal. Should she fake it? The
students certainly were easily hoodwinked. Perhaps she could
just nod and giggle at everything the principal said, pretending
to understand him, and he'd never know the difference. Very
risky, she concluded. Finally, Kay decided to bring a French-
English dictionary with her to the meeting and try to look up key
words quickly as the principal spoke them and try to respond to
the gist of his speech.

Too soon Kay sat across the desk from her new boss. Kay's tiny
dictionary lay hidden in her lap. The agile-looking Frenchman of
middle age, who sat before her, with his excellently tailored suit,
his smooth manners, and his suave good looks, far outstripped
the man who, only yesterday, occupied his desk. Although
nervous, Kay felt a certain attraction to her strange new boss.
She desired his approval.

"Madame Fortunata," the principal intoned. "Comme vous
le savez déjà, les méthodes d'éducation les plus modernes sont
toujours dans l'optique de Peale—"

Kay recognized the word "moderne" and responded in her
best movie-French, "Mais oui, monsieur."

"Alors," the principal continued, his brandy voice stirring
something pleasant deep inside of Kay. "Écoutez-moi. Nous
voulons créer une école dans une école—un concept très moderne.
L'objectif de cette petite école serait d'enseigner la couture. Grâce
à l'enseignement de la couture, les élèves apprendront beaucoup
plus. Qu'est-ce que vous pensez de cette idée d'un petit lycée de
la couture?"

Kay recognized the interrogative in the tone of this last
statement, and she sensed that "couture" was the important
term. Unfortunately, the principal had spoken so quickly and so
slurringly, as the French are apt to do, that poor Kay did not hear
"couture" correctly. Instead, she heard something like "prendre...
un petit coup." So she shot through her dictionary in a panic,
alighting finally on this phrase, "prendre un petit coup," which
the dictionary defined as a slang expression meaning something
like having a brief sexual episode, a quickie. Thus, Kay decided
that the principal had called her into his office to ask her for sex.

Finding this prospect not completely unappealing, Kay

smiled.

"Nous pensons que vous feriez un excellent directrice de ce programme," *the principal said.*

"Directrice...program," *thought Kay, understanding the French-English cognates. "What is this?" Kay wondered, "Does he want to put me in charge of arranging his quickies?" Kay's smile grew unsteady. She had to say something, but she was completely confused.*

Now, if Kay had been more conversant in French, she would have been overjoyed by the what the principal said; namely, that she had just been chosen as the director of the new petit lycée de la couture, *which had nothing to do with the principal's sex life, since a* petit lycée de la couture *is a "little school of needlework." The principal wanted to start a small school-within-a-school, a small learning community, if you will, and this school would be a school devoted to needlework, and he wanted to make Kay the boss. Unfortunately, all this passed right over Kay's head, which was too bad because it would have been the nicest thing that ever happened to her in her professional life.*

The debonair principal leaned toward Kay, awaiting a response to his offer to make her the administrator of a program, but Kay could only look at him and wonder.

Then, abruptly, the French substitute for Assistant Principal Price barged into the room and stammered, "Il y a une mêlée au réfectoire!" which means that there was a melee in the cafeteria.

The principal, hearing this, sprang from his desk, saying to Kay as he shot past her, "Réfléchissezons-y bien!" and both men ran out of the room together, leaving Kay bewildered.

Kay had mistaken the assistant principal's pronunciation of mêelée *for* melon, *and she wondered why the principal was so excited about "melons" in the cafeteria. She felt humiliated because first the principal seemed to have staged an elaborate seduction or put her in charge of his impromptu assignations, and then he had left her alone in favor of the melons in the cafeteria. In any event, her important meeting with the principal was over and she had accomplished nothing.*

Kay shrugged her shoulders and shook her head and, after a while, during which she sat and mumbled to herself, she picked up her big bag, which seemed to weigh more and more as the day went on. She trod off to her department office to spend the rest of the period. There, she slumped in a chair and awaited the bell, which would signal the time for her next class. She was so upset, she did not even feel like doing needlepoint. She kicked her knitting bag where it lay on the floor. Looking up, she saw her reflection in a mirror, and she looked as if she'd had a fight. Her hair was all undone.

Kay confronted her grief. She wondered how long she could fake teaching in a foreign language. Could she get along speaking her meaningless English? She wondered how she could even talk to a colleague who might walk into the office or someone who might call on the phone. She considered retiring immediately, in spite of the fact that this would condemn her to a life of poverty. Ultimately, she realized that she was the foreigner; that she was the freak, and with this she gave herself up to grief. She sobbed, "I want my school back!" Her eyes glistened with water, and a big tear rolled down her cheek. Then she slumped forward toward a desk and wept convulsively, her head buried in her hands.

She cried for some time. She cried through the rest of the day. She cried as she taught the rest of her classes, which went no worse than the previous classes. She cried until she ran out of tears. When the dismissal bell rang, and the halls filled with the exuberant babble of French youth, Kay made up her mind about what to do. She lifted her head, and picked up her bag. She walked through the door with her head high; her mind was clear; her eyes were dry. She would learn to speak French. It would take a while, during which she would have to do a bit of faking, but she would be OK. She was good with languages. She would teach Molière and Hugo, Zola and Flaubert, Sartre and Camus. Why not? Literature is literature, only the words are different. She would buy a Berlitz on the way home. By tomorrow she would be saying "Bonjour!" and "Ça va?" In a few weeks, she would be communicating like a pro—in French. Everything would be fine.

On her way out of the school, Kay stopped at her mailbox and looked through her letters and memos. This mail shook her newfound confidence a little. The mail was very odd. It didn't seem French at all. And it certainly was not English. The alphabet in which the letters were written was fraught with odd diacritical marks. She could make neither heads nor tails of the writing. She turned toward a colleague and asked, "What language are these letters written in?" But the man she addressed, whom she did not *recognize, and who wore a long scarf, and was actually smoking a cigarette in the school building, just looked at her as though she were nuts. "Ja nie rozumiem," said the stranger. Kay looked at her letters. She looked at the stranger. He held his cigarette between his thumb and forefinger like a dart and drew the smoke from it deeply, as though it were his last cigarette on earth. He exhaled a cloud of smoke that covered Kay. Standing in this veil of smoke, she realized what had happened. She could hear it in the hallways. She could see it in the face of her strange colleague. Everyone was speaking Polish. Everyone was now Polish....*

Mrs. Worthington sat with her elbow on the table and her chin in her hand. One finger tapped her cheek. "Uh huh," she said.

"No lie," said Wood. And he arose, "Now, I've got to get over to the library to book the computer room." And he gathered his things and left.

"What do you suppose prompted that story?" I asked.

"I think it was the Observation," said Worthington.

"Doubtless," I said. I noticed there were a few minutes left in the period. I thought I might take a leisurely trip to the men's room, have a piss, and listen to my colleagues pee. This was a pastime I sometimes pursued to make myself feel better about getting older and pissing poorly myself. Some of the older gentlemen on the staff had a terrible time, and I felt better when I heard their feeble efforts.

I pocketed my recorder, congratulating myself on capturing Wood's story and certain it would prove useful to me. This acquisition made up for the distress I'd suffered at the hands of Miss Rigg, and it had allowed me to forget about Ms. Schlect—and her evil shoes, and more evil clipboard—for a while. I'd repress that Rigg thing by fifth period, I thought, and I'd check out what Mr. Wood was doing with *The Metamorphosis* during sixth.

As I packed my things, getting ready to go, Worthington glanced my way and asked, "By the way, have you heard from the principal?"

"The principal? About what?"

Worthington hesitated, as though she were not supposed to have spoken.

"What is it?" I asked.

"I may as well tell you. You're going to find out soon enough.

But don't tell anyone that I told you."

"What?"

Worthington's fork held a chunk of chicken doused in dressing. "A student in one of your classes accused you of cheating on the last benchmark test."

"Cheating? Me? A student..."

"Well, actually, his parent accused you. And she didn't call the school with the accusation; she called the Administration office downtown."

"Wha... Wha... Who's the student?" I asked. "What did he say I did? I don't remember cheating on a test."

"I don't know anything else," said Worthington. "Since I am the testing coordinator, I was in the meeting when this came up. Your name was mentioned. The business of cheating was brought up. But I heard no specifics. Calm down. I'm sure it's nothing. The principal will call you. Just don't tell him I told you about this. I don't think I was supposed to."

"What are the consequences?" I asked.

"I don't know. I don't even know what you did. But there is a whole section on the subject of inappropriate behavior on the part of the proctor in the *Administrator's Guide Book* I put in your mailbox. You read the guide, right?"

"Of course," I lied.

7. Mrs. Kessler, Franz Kafka, and Barack Obama

PEOPLE at work always found it strange that I referred to my wife as "Mrs. Kessler," instead of "Lois" or "my wife," or something a bit more endearing than "Mrs. Kessler." I had two reasons for this: First, like me, she was a teacher and, therefore, Mrs. Kessler was her professional name, and this made it a perfectly acceptable moniker. Secondly, she and I were not really on what you might call a first-name basis, so "Mrs. Kessler" was what I was comfortable calling her. Fact is, I hadn't spoken to Mrs. Kessler in close to fifteen years. That is, I hadn't spoken to her beyond small utilitarian phrases like, "Do you have anything else for the trash before I take it down?" or "Could you hand me the television listings?" She responded to me similarly, briefly and to the point, and this was OK with me since this kind of superficial dialogue precluded any arguments.

Mrs. Kessler stopped talking to me after a huge fight we had fifteen years ago, which had ended in my slapping her in the face, which I regret to this day, and I have no idea how I got to the point where I would do such a thing. The fight escalated from a disagreement we had over where to spend a bit of money we'd saved. She claimed that the money was earmarked for a vacation to Europe, and I insisted that we should use the money to remodel our leaky bathroom. I suppose we might have worked this out somehow—it was not a big deal at first—but I made the mistake of going ahead and hiring a contractor and buying all the materials for the remodeling project behind Mrs. Kessler's back. This made her angry, even though she had already gone behind my back and scheduled flights to Europe and booked rooms. One day, unbeknownst to Mrs. Kessler, a contractor showed up and demolished the bathroom while we both were at work—I'd left a key under the welcome mat for him—and when Mrs. Kessler came home and found the repairs underway, she was upset—is that the word, "upset"? Maybe "furious" is better—and the idea that she had no bathroom to use for two weeks—except the half-bath in the basement—didn't help. When the contractor (and his assistant, who looked like a criminal—which also didn't help) left that evening, Mrs. Kessler and I had words. My argument was that it was far more important to keep one's house in repair than it was to take a frivolous trip, which would end in a few weeks and leave us with nothing but memories. To this day I do not regret my position. But I do regret smacking Mrs. Kessler when she informed me that she'd sunk a considerable amount of money into hotel deposits and plane fares and wasn't sure she could get it all back. I gave her a short, backhanded slap—nothing violent, mind you—and I remember her turning crimson, and thinking for a moment about whether to strike me back or not, and then stalking off and crying.

We might have mended our fences except, after a few weeks of silence, Mrs. Kessler retaliated for her slap by bringing home a fully-grown Shar Pei that became the bane of my existence for the next few years until the poor dog died of one of the multifarious (and expensive) ailments to which it was prone and which caused it to stink like low tide and shed like a truck full of hay. What a pip that dog was! Besides being incontinent, which made me an expert at cleaning dog puddles from the carpet, this dog, whose name was Betty, ate everything in sight. She ate candles as though they were candy. She ate throw pillows, figurines, kitchen gadgets, all the medications she could find, and she particularly loved paper. She would eat your homework in a trice. I think she ate a curtain once, because she pulled the curtains down and one panel was missing. I never took her outside for a walk, but I assume her defecations were full of buttons, gears, and shards. She may have been part goat. Betty was allowed, against my protest, to roam free all day while we were at work, and Mrs. Kessler exacted a cruel revenge through the antics of her dog, though my impression was that Mrs. Kessler was hoisted on her own petard by Betty, who needed constant care and the attention of a full-time vet. Anyhow, Betty sealed the deal on our mutual silence. After Betty, Mrs. Kessler and I lived together, but alone. We resorted to less violent, more reserved retaliations. I separated my bank account from hers. She withdrew into a separate bedroom. I stopped doing her heavy lifting.

Perhaps most disconcerting, she joined a cult of some kind—a group of pagans. An exotic altar appeared in her room, and on this altar she burned candles and incense at the feet of graven idols. Wearing a black cape, she disappeared from home four times a year, on the evenings of the solstices and equinoxes. And one spring solstice she invited her coven to our home, where they assembled in her room—before her altar, I expect (the door was closed), and they chanted in unison. Driven by curiosity, I held my ear to her door to determine the nature of their chants, and I was astonished to hear that they were worshiping the Greek goddess Persephone. I had read this myth in English classes with students many times, but I certainly never dreamed that cults devoted to this goddess still existed. This really sealed the deal on our mutual avoidance of one another. I was sure Mrs. Kessler joined this outrageous group of idol worshippers out of spite. Prowling through her room one evening while she was out, I found a little puppet with a bald head, just like mine, and there was a hat pin sticking in its ass in exactly the same spot where I'd recently developed a sharp sciatic pain. This was the final evidence that showed me that we'd grown irreparably apart.

In keeping with my resolution to tell the truth, I suppose I have to answer some questions at this point: No, Mrs. Kessler and I had not had sex for many years. Yes, we had, still have, a child, a boy named Henry—I call him Hank—who left for college in Massachusetts when he was eighteen and never returned. He may or may not be a homosexual, but he lives with a male roommate in Boston where he makes a living as a pastry chef. We haven't seen him in years. No, Mrs. Kessler and I never discussed divorce— never brought the subject up—too financially dependent on one another, and while Hank was at home we were both devoted to him. And, finally, no, I have never—not then not now—felt lonely or in need of intimacy. Except right before bed, sometimes. When it's time to turn in, in my lonely room, in my empty bed, I have often thought, just before getting under the covers, it would be nice to have someone to say a few words to.... For a while before sleeping, I do feel lonely. Perhaps it's because sleep is a little like death—*death's second self, that seals up all in rest*—and no one wants to die alone, they say.

All this, which I would rather not have included in this story, is just to show how disturbed I was after I found out that someone had accused me of cheating on the benchmark test. My annoyance over this even superseded my feelings about my separation from Mrs. Kessler and my impending Observation.

That evening, after Worthington indicated that the principal would contact me, while I was sipping my martini in the breakfast nook and Mrs. Kessler was washing vegetables in the sink, I actually confided in her about my problem, something I hadn't done in many years. That's how upset I was. She turned and looked at me suspiciously, wondering what I was up to.

"You got caught cheating on a benchmark? How did you cheat?" she asked.

"I don't know yet," I said. "I'm supposed to have a meeting with the principal and find out, but I don't know when."

"I mean, were you giving out answers or altering answer sheets?"

"Dear God, no,"

"And you don't remember cheating?"

"I honestly don't."

"Well, now that's hilarious," she said, "I was at a District meeting recently where a number of teachers were comparing notes on how they cheat on tests. They do it flagrantly. Sometimes, before they turn in the answer sheets, they change a bunch of answers. Sometimes they walk around the room and coach kids during the test. Sometime they give a few answers away before the test begins if they think the questions are too hard...."

"I never did anything like that," I said. "Our students generally do pretty well on these tests without help."

"Yeah, well, if you teach in a school where the students don't do well, it's in your best interest to cheat, because God knows what the powers-that-be will do to you or your school if your school doesn't show progress. Why, I've even heard stories of principals *requiring* teachers to cheat." Mrs. Kessler turned back to the sink and chuckled, saying, "But no one gets caught. Whoever heard of getting caught?" She laughed so loud her laughter echoed in the sink.

I indulged in an extra martini with dinner that night. I needed to medicate a nagging pain in my upper back and to forget a day of monumental emotional—and respiratory—distress, distress so deep I'd actually shown it to Mrs. K, hoping for consolation.

The extra martini I drank, though, let me down. It spawned in my brain a legion of phantasms while I tried to watch television that night. The specter of the angry principal tormented me. Then, haunted by fears, I had no rest—just rolled around in a sweaty twilight-sleep while the same thought-dream repeated itself over and over. In the dream, I was fired from teaching for cheating, and no one cared. There was no student protest, no union grievance, no administrative intervention. My peers were indifferent. Rigg was overjoyed. I saw myself replaced by a younger person, someone who cost considerably less to maintain, and everyone loved this person as they did not love me. My students entered class the day after I was terminated, and they cheered. They sent up the same cheer as when a substitute stepped in for me. I imagined administrators and secretaries joking while my mailbox was replaced. My fellow teachers, even my new lunch buddies, sent me no words of consolation. I was forgotten in a day, an hour. I was like Scrooge imagining his death and the lack of concern it caused. Then I imagined my pension was revoked, and this thought worked my brain like the dripping of a leaky faucet.

The next day, I was in a kind of trance. I could feel a cramp gelling in my chest during the first two periods. My heart was missing beats. Third period came and Miss Rigg did not speak to me (though she'd replaced the things on my desk by the time I had returned on the previous day). Remarkably, her class filed in quietly and sat in their places—except Gus, whom Rigg, when she arrived, disarmed with a simple, "Gus! Sit."—and the class proceeded without the usual negotiation.

I nodded at Rigg and hurried to the English office. Because I had settled on the idea of copying one of Wood's lessons when I was observed, I needed to find out what part he was up to in *The Metamorphosis*. I thought I might ask him what he was doing, knowing he'd be more than happy to explain, and this would allow me to rest my hangover during sixth period instead of eavesdropping on him.

When Wood arrived he brought forth, from a stained paper bag, an unprecedented tuna hoagie. He unpackaged the sandwich and ran his eyes over the soggy Italian roll stuffed with runny tuna salad. It filled the room with the gamey smell of fish. Because the tomatoes and onions that topped the tuna sat perpendicular to the crease of the sandwich, Wood had to squeeze them inside the bread with a plastic knife, and a river of tuna juice ran onto the plastic wrap he used as a plate. My hangover found this sandwich most unappetizing. My stomach turned a hundred and eighty degrees. I moved my lunch aside and forgot all about Kafka.

Coincidentally, Wood himself resurrected the haunted Czech. After pushing a goodly portion of the stinky hoagie into his mouth, he said, his mouth full, "Franz Kafka is the man."

"Why the man?" I asked. Queasy as I was, for the first time all year one of Wood's literary discussions piqued my interest.

"I asked my students to interpret the symbol of the bug in *The Metamorphosis*."

Symbol of the bug...symbol of the bug, I couldn't imagine what he was talking about. Damn that gin. "Good idea," I said.

"But I didn't tell them what *I* think the bug represents. I'm leaving it all up to them. I just told them at the beginning of the reading that our whole task in reading this novella is to interpret the symbol of the bug. What do you think?"

I thought, *You're whistling in the dark. The meaning of the bug is clear. Kafka felt like his family treated him like a bug. His father especially. So he made himself into a bug in the story and made his father a person who is revolted by the bug. Problem solved. I hate bugs myself.* But I said, "Symbol of the bug...symbol of the bug. Let them figure it out...."

"The bug could represent," Wood chomped on that awful sandwich with his mouth open and a napkin at the ready, "all the things that might *cause* alienation in a family. It could represent sickness. A family like Gregor's, a careless family, would resent a member who is sick and draining the family's resources." Wood wiped a drop of mayo from the corner of his mouth. "...It could represent unemployment. Gregor has to quit his job, making him an economic blight—a bug! It could even represent artistic freedom, or a bohemian lifestyle, since Gregor is doing his own thing as a bug... How about depression, debilitating depression? Or simply being a writer? I picture Gregor, the human-size bug, leaning on the window sill, totally despondent, gazing out at the rain and the mean streets of Prague, with the stark hospital across the street, and seeing his former self, the stressed salesman, marching off...to what, emptiness?"

"Bugs are annoying," I said, feeling greener than ever, looking at Wood's tuna-soaked sandwich.

"Gregor is like Bartleby, alienated from society, but pitiable."

"Gregor is sympathetic?"

Mrs. Worthington entered. "What are you talking about?" she asked, "I love *Bartleby the Scrivener*. I teach it every year."

"I'm comparing Bartleby to Gregor Samsa," Wood said.

"I can see that," said Worthington, sitting. "You look awful," she said to me. "Out last night?"

"Didn't sleep. Paul's sandwich doesn't help."

Mr. Wood chuckled, "Mmmm-mmm," he said. "Yummy." He licked the mayo off his fingers.

I abandoned my idea to ask Wood for a lesson. If I did, I would have to listen to more of his pontificating on symbolism and alienation, or whatever. So I reverted to the idea of eavesdropping on his class later in the day, during my preparation period and checking things out. I would just pray that Frau Schlect would not visit me between now and then. Meanwhile, my brain was a bit too fuzzy to join in the conversation between Wood and Worthington. They were discussing politics, a subject that rankled me, especially since the election of Barack Obama. They were talking about health care reform. Worthington took the position that it was about time the government got around to addressing the availability of health care and its expense, and Wood was complaining that there were so many conflicts of interest he doubted that the reforms would have any teeth. My half-consciousness repeated the mantra it always did during such an argument: The government never does anything right, so just let the system work on its own. I thought, *That Obama is always trying to give the store away. Where is Ronald Reagan when we need him?* But I said, "Leave it to Obama. He'll do the right thing."

8. Mission aborted

BY SIXTH period, I was in serious need of a rest. Normally, on a day after I'd treated myself to an extra martini and I was feeling low, during my preparation period, I'd go to the area of the men's room where there was a couch and lie down, maybe even catch forty winks. On this day, I was woozy and my heart had been acting funny all day and a lie-down would certainly help. But I was resolved to spy on Mr. Wood, at least for half the period, to pick up a lesson or at least an idea for a lesson on *The Metamorphosis*. However, sixth period, just as I was leaving on my mission to Wood's, I was interrupted.

A student entered my room and told me the principal would like to see me. "Dr. Hirshburg is not happy that your phone isn't working," the boy, a member of the student government, said. I often kept the phone off the hook to preclude having to answer it while I was teaching. A classroom phone might ring three or four times during a period, and it was a major inconvenience to stop what I was doing and answer the phone. "He told me to tell you to hurry," said the student. A summons from the principal usually precipitated a heart palpitation, and this was no exception, even though I was expecting his summons. My heart stopped for a full second and then pounded. I'd have to put off harvesting a lesson from Wood, and I'd have to pray harder for Ms. Schlect to delay her Observation.

On my way to the principal's office, I experienced a debilitating esophageal cramp to complement my intermittent heart palpitations, and I swore I was experiencing an actual heart attack, so I ducked into the men's room to rest for a spell, regardless of the consequences. When I opened the door to enter, there was an old man in there, someone I didn't recognize—a small, hunched, ancient old creature in coveralls, with dirty hair that hung like worms to his shoulders. He was doing something with his back turned, I couldn't tell what, maybe fixing something or unscrewing the lid of a difficult jar. He was making a kind of creaking sound, almost like crying...so I didn't stay.

In the principal's office, I saw my department chair, Mrs. Hegel, sitting in one corner of the room, and I saw the principal behind his desk working on a cup of coffee, and there was a stranger standing behind a chair—an albino man with white hair and pink eyes. The principal bade me sit and introduced the albino man as Mr. Latovick. Latovick was grasping the back of the chair he stood behind so tightly the knuckles on his pink hands were bloodless.

I bowed quickly and sat.

The principal said something about wanting to dispose of this case simply and without harm to anyone. He asked me if I would forgo union representation at this time in an effort to expedite the case quickly, here and now, and I agreed. He mentioned that a parent had called the Office of Assessment with a complaint about me, and Mr. Latovick was here to investigate. Then he nodded at Latovick, giving him the floor.

"Good day, Mr. Kessler," said Latovick. He seemed impatient and spoke quickly.

"Good day, sir."

"Let me get right to the point. On the morning of January 10, when you were administrating the second benchmark examination to your second period class of tenth graders, did you give the class any information about the test beyond the instructions?"

"I don't remember," I said. All eyes were on me. Especially unsettling were the pink eyes of Latovick. He licked his pale lips with his narrow tongue, and his eyelids became half moons fringed with tiny blond spikes. My cramp reached a plateau. I sat up very straight in an effort to control the pain.

"Let me be more specific," said the rabbit-eyed Latovick,

circling his chair like a lawyer, unbuttoning his jacket, and taking a seat. He pointed at me. "Did you give the class the definition of the word 'fiasco' before you administered the test?"

Uh oh, I thought. I did do that. There was a reading selection on the test that contained the word "fiasco," and it didn't use the word to mean a "disaster" or a "debacle;" the question used the word to describe a wine bottle with a basket covering. I assumed no student would know what a fiasco was—not when it referred to a wine bottle, even if a few students might know the "disaster" definition. So, before the test began, I told the class what a fiasco was.

"Well..." I said, trying to find a position to alleviate my chest cramp.

But before I committed to an answer, I weighed the benefits of lying against the benefits of telling the truth—always a difficult consideration, especially when something important is at stake. Lying is a gamble. It might work and absolve one's crime immediately. But, if the interrogator thinks the criminal is lying, he might try to expose the lie by asking more questions. This necessitates further lies on the part of the liar, until his lies become so entangled and inconsistent he stands a good chance of exposing himself. Then the lies themselves become a crime and compound, and even overshadow, the original crime—the cover-up is worse than the original crime. Was Latovick smart enough to expose the truth? That was the question... Telling the truth, on the other hand, could possibly satisfy the interrogator, and that might be the end of it. In a case where the crime is not worth the gamble of the lie, the truth is the best policy. And yet, the truth is a gamble, also, because it may invite an inordinate punishment without any chance of escape. The criminal does not know what the punishment will be as long as he does not know the intentions of the prosecutor. And I certainly didn't know anyone like Latovick, whose wet lips and pale flesh gave him the appearance of a white lizard that lived without sunlight....

I looked for help from the principal and my department chair, but there was none forthcoming. The cramp in my esophagus (or heart attack) continued, and I pressed my hand to my chest. Latovick leaned forward impatiently, his hand feeling for something in his pocket, and I decided that he very was serious about his job, and he would give me the third degree if I lied and said I did not define "fiasco." My chest hurt and I needed to get out of this situation as soon as possible, so I resolved to gamble with the truth. After all, the word "fiasco" was not even important to any of the questions on the test. It was just a part of a reading selection. I didn't want to take any chances with Latovick, who was inching forward by the moment, growing pinker and pinker, and seeming to breathe through his neck.

"...Yes," I said. "I did define 'fiasco' for the class."

"Ah-ha!" Latovick sprang from his place and pointed at me. "That's cheating! That's cheating!" he cried, and rounded again to the back of his chair to catch his breath. He looked at the ceiling, "He cheated," he said with triumph, grasping the back of the chair and looking up toward the gods of test administration while he rebuttoned his jacket.

The principal said something about being happy to get to the bottom of the matter, hoping to resolve the issue at once. And my department chair registered a complaint about the numerous poorly worded questions on the test. But Latovick was not listening. He loaded another question. "When your student, Thomas Salter, said to you that talking about the test was illegal and asked you if he could leave the room while you talked, did you send him out?" Latovick locked me in his bizarre pink stare once more, and he squeezed the back of the chair as though he wanted to strangle it.

Uh oh, I thought, I did that too. Salter, a quiet and industrious kid, asked to leave the room when I defined "fiasco" because, he said, he didn't want to be present if I were giving out answers. I remembered teasing him, calling him a goodie-goodie, telling him that defining "fiasco" was hardly cheating, and sending him to the bathroom. Then, when he came back, I did not give him extra time for the test, although he missed a few minutes, because, after all, he had questioned my authority.

The cramp in my chest reached a new apex. This time when I considered the benefits of lying versus the benefits of telling the truth, I lied and said, "No, I did no such thing."

Latovick was disappointed because this matter of sending a student out of the room so I could continue cheating was, by far, the worse crime, and it would make his case against me much more convincing. He unbuttoned his jacket, assumed his seat, and asked a few more questions, but I shut myself up like a clam, saying, "I don't remember" to everything. And finally Latovick said to the principal that there would have to be another meeting, this time with a member of the Assessment Office's legal team. He leaned back in his chair, gazing down his nose at me, and he spoke solemnly, "Cheating on a benchmark test is not an insignificant offense. There are people in Harrisburg who would be very interested in this case." And I thought: *Harrisburg! I wouldn't mind being fired; I had my forty years in. But could my pension be at stake?*

I was about to defend myself by explaining how insignificant I thought my crime was compared with cases that I had heard about—teachers all over the District giving out answers and changing answer sheets...

But the principal's intuition told him he needed to shut me up, and he said, "Mr. Kessler, don't say another word until you contact your union," cutting me short. I was excused, and I staggered back to my room to teach my last two classes. Spying on Wood was out of the question.

Then the worst possible thing happened. Soon after last period began, Ms. Schlect clickity-clicked into my room to observe my class. The heels of her shoes were so high they reminded me of the pilings that hold up a pier, and in her arms she cradled her infernal clipboard. She smiled brightly and sat in the back of the room. The boy in front of her turned and looked down at her bright red, shiny shoes, and when he turned back toward the front he wore a goofy smile. I was tired and breathless and, though the cramp in my chest had subsided, I was shaken by the events of the day and fearful of further symptoms, so I walked to the back of the room and told Ms. Schlect that now was not a good time for my Observation, but she said she would only stay a few minutes.

"You're such a senior member of the staff," she said. "You don't require much watching."

Since I didn't have time to prepare the lesson I wanted to show her, I had to revert to my regularly scheduled plan, which was hardly a plan at all, just a short grammar drill followed by students reading out loud from *The Metamorphosis*.

Missy Brooks, who had recently informed me that she was pregnant, fell asleep during the reading, and she was sitting next to Ms. Schlect. Though this made me nervous, I ignored Missy until Mike Quinn, who had recently traded his ponytail for a buzz cut, put his head down on the desk, and I thought I'd better intervene before snoozing became epidemic. I asked Missy if she were sick, and she said yes. So I had to spend some time writing a note for her to take to the nurse, during which time the class fell into general confusion, which I quelled with a threat to lower the grades of the talkers. Then I asked Mike if he were sick, and he reluctantly lifted his head and said, "This is so boring." Another student agreed, saying, "This book is terrible. Let's read something else." I got a little angry and assured the class that a book like *The Metamorphosis*, a classic, which had withstood the test of time, could not be terrible or it would have disappeared. Then I threatened to lower the grade of any student who spoke out of turn with a critical remark about the literature. This elicited a short chorus of groans and some laughter. During which, the fellow in front of Ms. Schlect turned for another gander at her shoes, and this time Ms. Schlect saw the need to physically turn his head back around for him. There was uneasiness in the class that I interpreted as an effort to appeal to Ms. Schlect for assistance in scrapping *The Metamorphosis*. So I mustered all my strength and, struggling to breathe, commanded the next reader to continue reading. After that portion there ensued a discussion about the size of Gregor the bug, and when we established that the bug was as big as a human, the class veered out of control talking among themselves about what they would do if they confronted a big bug. I heard the following remarks, in no particular order:

"I'd run. Bugs eat anything."

"You'd better run; bugs land on shit."

"Did you see the *The Fly*, where this scientist gets drunk and turns himself into a fly?"

"Spiderman fights the Fly."

"I hate bugs. They're ugly."

"We call Lance 'Bug;' look at his eyes."

"Shut up!"

As the class pursued this line of discussion, Ms. Schlect scribbled continuously. I felt my esophagus beginning to twist again and a sharp pain in my upper back. I moved aside from my podium so the students could see I was making threatening marks in my gradebook—I no longer had the strength to shout—and they settled down.

I was careful not to stop the reading for any further discussion, and we read together for the last half hour of the class. I heard the clickity-clack of Ms. Schlect's heels when she removed herself from the room just before the bell for dismissal. I was sad to note, when I looked up from my text, that there were no fewer than four sleepers in the room. They roused themselves to go to their next class. Lisa Wong, who had paid attention throughout the class, said, quite cheerfully, "Bye, Mr. K."

9. Channels of communication

I RECEIVED a note from young Ms. Schlect the next day saying she was seriously considering rating me as "unsatisfactory" as a result of her Observation but, before she did that (the note proceeded in italics), she would permit me to undergo another Observation in two weeks' time (she indicated the exact date and period she would arrive) and, if I could "execute a lesson that is aligned with the curriculum and prevoked (sic) intrinsic motivation" she would see clear to forget this first Observation and file the second.

Even though I should not have, I went home after my bad day with the abysmal Mr. Latovick and the torturous Ms. Schlect and again dived into a large martini. I did not even bother pouring the drink into a glass but stood at the kitchen counter and drank it directly from the metal shaker. Afterward, I staggered to the couch where I collapsed into a sleep so deep it seemed as if I'd been tossed from a ship with my hands tied behind my back and had sunk to the bottom of the ocean.

Mrs. Kessler woke me, saying it was dinnertime and I was snoring so loud it frightened her. She recommended that I should ask the doctor for a sleep study since I stopped breathing a few times while I was unconscious. I stumbled into the kitchen for dinner.

I remember a time when Mrs. Kessler was devoted to the practice of cooking. Every afternoon, when she came home from work, she donned her apron and entered a private world for an hour and a half (while I drank). She made homemade tater tots and topped them with caviar and sour cream; she made her own delicate ravioli stuffed with crab and gorgonzola; she deep fried lotus root dredged in panko. I remember coming home from school and finding a whole fish that twitched on the kitchen counter now, but soon would be swimming in puttanesca; her smothered pork chops made you ditch your fork and pick up the chops and get your fingers greasy; she put a mushroom button and a bit of buttery brown gravy on a steak; she garnished things.... But that was a lifetime ago, and now she specialized in only one food—tofu. It was all tofu all the time. She stir-fried tofu with vegetables or mixed tofu with spaghetti or set a few rubbery cubes of the stuff next to a salmon filet that she baked unadorned. Her most adventurous cooking nowadays was a tofu pizza, made with strange ersatz cheese. I guess I was lucky she still cooked for me at all.

In the good old days I topped off Mrs. Kessler's gourmet dinners with ice cream every night. I loved ice cream so much I thought about it during the day as one might fantasize about sex in an idle moment. Yes, dinner was something in those days—imagine: martini, pork chops, ice cream, more martini... every night. What a deal! Something to live for! And there were sandwiches, like Wood's, in the afternoon, and Mrs. Kessler made them and packed them in a brown bag with a pickle and some chips. And there were late-night snacks, cold leftovers that demanded to be consumed to the bottom of the container... But that was sixty pounds and a hundred doctors' lectures ago. Now it was a banana, an apple, a snack bar (thank God for the snack bar), and those endless cubes of bean curd. No cigarettes, no coffee, no dessert. But I guarded the martinis jealously; they'd have to pry the martini glass from my cold, dead fingers.

I confided in Mrs. Kessler when we sat down to our dinner of fried tofu (which was reasonably satisfying because it was spicy) and vegetables. "I had my meeting with the principal," I said.

"And?"

"There was this guy from the Board there, from the Office of Assessment. He was a terrible man, more like a creature from under the earth than a man. He said a parent had lodged a complaint against me—that I defined a word on the test before I gave the test. I had to admit it. I had defined the word. And when I admitted it, he jumped out of his seat and pointed a finger at me and said, 'That's cheating, that's cheating, that's cheating!' He got all excited."

Mrs. Kessler asked me to review what I had done on the day of the test, and she asked for more details about the meeting in the principal's office, and I filled her in completely. She said, "It's not like you to tell the truth. So what's next?"

I told her that I would need union representation for the next meeting and that Latovick would bring a lawyer from the Board.

Mrs. Kessler considered this a propitious time to give me a piece of news that, under different circumstances, she might have left unsaid. She may have chosen this moment because, with my talk about my problem at school, I had opened a channel of communication that had not existed between us for some time. On the other hand, she may have chosen this moment because I seemed vulnerable and she could cause the most pain. I don't know. In any event, she normally would have proceeded with her plans in secret and allowed the outcome to be a surprise, but she opened up instead. To her credit, she began her speech in a gentle way, and then dropped her bombs. "You must be really stressed from your trouble at work," she said, placing a hand on mine (and I may have flinched). "But it will probably blow over. I don't think you need to worry. You know, you can retire at any time. You've got how many years?"

"Thirty-nine and a half."

"That's plenty. I don't know why you keep going back.... Anyhow, this might not be the best time to tell you this, and I'm sorry for telling you while you have other worries, but I'm leaving. I'm moving out. I have my own place. I'll be gone in two months."

It does not say much for me that her words did not affect me too far beyond the financial considerations. "Can you afford to live alone?" I asked. She took her hand away and said she could, that she had it all worked out, and that she had contacted a lawyer to get advice about our separating or divorcing.

I considered for a moment that she might have found someone, a lover. She was no longer the fat woman who was married to a fat man and who must, therefore, sit hopelessly on the sidelines in the game of love. She'd lost more weight than I. And to consider that her devotion to me would hold her back from the pursuit of love was absurd. She was available. But I saw very little to commend her in the eyes of a lover. Her years of obesity had left her shapeless, just as her years of being loveless had left her dowdy, and she long ago lost the habits of making up her face or fussing over her hair. I think she cut her own hair and let the grey hairs flourish. No, I decided, she had no boyfriend, and that was just as well for him because she was, after all, ornery enough to bring a leaky dog into her own home just for spite. I ruled out the idea of a lover.

I did not respond to Mrs. Kessler's news, just dropped the whole subject of her leaving and cut off the channel of communication. Responding would have led to a long and laborious conversation—something I didn't want. Instead, I headed for the metal container and the ice cube tray, and rarely did the clink-clink of the ice and the glug-glug of the gin sound better.

I now regret that I did not ask Mrs. K her reasons for leaving, and I regret that I spent the remainder of the night more worried about my impending meeting with Latovick and his lawyer than the end of my marriage. I really should have said something to Mrs. K—to sort of finish things. When I trudged off to bed that night, I could hear Mrs. Kessler weeping quietly in her room across the hall. But still, I did not respond.

10. Schadenfreude and the big administrators

EARLY the next morning, at my desk in school, I noticed that my scissors were missing from the drawer where I normally kept them. I could not tell exactly when the theft occurred because I rarely used scissors. But in my delicate state of mind, I was shaken—even more than usual. After rummaging through my drawers in search of the missing scissors, I sprang from my chair and paced back and forth in the front of my room, talking to myself and thinking what to do. I considered bringing the matter to the attention of Miss Rigg again, but discreetly this time. Who else could be the culprit, except she or one of the students for whom she was responsible? I'd followed Wood's advice and kept a careful watch on my room, locking it whenever I was not there, and only during the period when Miss Rigg was in charge could there possibly have been a theft. *But, oh,* I thought, *to confront Miss Rigg again would take courage.*

I was unable to resolve this issue because grades were soon due, and I needed to finish grading a stack of tests and compile all the scores in my computer. Four times a year, a teacher must calculate a grade for each of his hundred and fifty students. This involves doing an arithmetic average for each kid, based on the twenty-five or thirty assignments the teacher has assigned in the quarter. When I first started teaching, we calculated an average for each student longhand, with a pencil and paper, and this was a major chore. The pocket calculator was a godsend, shaving a dozen hours. But when I discovered, midway through my career, that there was a computer program that would calculate all my grades for me, I almost cried. I hugged the man who showed it to me, and wouldn't let him go. It was the reason I bought my first computer, an old Apple IIe. I reckon that this grading program saved me more than fifty hours a year in tedious mathematical calculations and was a major weapon in my campaign to finish all my school work in school. Northwest provided me with a jazzy MacBook laptop, which I used primarily to prepare grades. Mr. Wood might use his computer coupled with a projector (that he bought) to adorn his speeches with pictures and graphs, or show his students how to design newspapers and slide shows, and otherwise employ this blessed machine to increase his workload but, as far as I was concerned, the computer was invented to save time and energy, and the ability to calculate grades effortlessly was its finest educational achievement.

Later in the day, I would prowl around Wood's class and gather some ideas for an acceptably fancy lesson on *The Metamorphosis* to satisfy the critical Ms. Schlect, but for now, I needed to sit down, crunch numbers, and make up grades. I decided that my lesson for the day would be to give my students a portion of *The Metamorphosis* to read silently, and then they would have to take a comprehension test on what they read, and this would keep them busy during class while I finished compiling their grades. I dashed off a quick true-or-false test, and I resumed compiling grades.

During the first two periods of the day, a paranoiac suspicion that Frau Schlect might peek in and catch me conducting busy-work distracted me slightly, but my silent-reading plan worked well enough (I ignored some cheating in the back of the room), and I was way ahead of the grading game by second period and dreaming of a frosty martini at day's end. By the time Miss Rigg and her class displaced me, my grades were just about up to date.

Miss Rigg's students entered like sheep before she showed up, and I wondered what that riot act she'd issued must have included. They filed in and sat, conversing in low tones. When Miss Rigg entered, she was wearing what looked like a red bandolier or sash, and I thought I might make a comment like, *Miss Rigg, you look swell today; you have a very sweet class. I can't imagine that there could be a bad egg among them but....* Or, *Beautiful sash, Miss Rigg! You know I left my scissors in this drawer, silver scissors about yay long, and...* But while I was arranging the fruit in my briefcase, and thinking of what I would say to Miss Rigg, I turned toward her and bumped my still-open laptop with my elbow. This might not have tipped the computer off my desk except, in reaching for it, I stepped on the power cord and that finished the job of toppling it. The computer fell from my desk onto the floor and landed directly on its edge with an alarming *cronk*. The battery spun out, and the screen separated from its frame. A terrible crack opened above the keyboard, and I thought it might bleed.

I panicked, not so much because I'd broken a computer—after all, it belonged to the school—so much as because I lost all the grades I'd just entered—mountains of data—and there was no backup copy. I'd stopped backing up my grade program when I'd lost the little flash drive that went missing from my desk. Miss Rigg looked at me as though I just committed a felony, and I'm sure I looked back at her with commensurate guilt.

I stooped and picked up the dead machine. I tapped its keys, but it did not respond to any commands. I replaced the battery, which would not stay in its place without my holding it there, but the battery gave it no life. I'd killed it, and with it I'd killed any chance of creating a justifiable grade for any of my one hundred and fifty students. I would have to make up their grades off the top of my head. And this would be an arbitrary grade indeed, since I had no writing assignments, which might have given me insights into my students' skills. Only tests, lots of tests, with numerical grades on them, almost all of which I'd returned to my students long ago. It occurred to me how little I actually knew about my students from my collection of test scores. Now I would have to give all of my students an overly generous grade, to preclude their complaining, because I now had no way to justify a grade to a student or his parent. I would have to give the worst students a "C," even if they had missed a considerable number of tests. I had no choice.

I looked up to see Miss Rigg looking down at me and my broken computer with some compassion and, looking up the other way, I saw Gus smiling down at me with amusement. Pointing to where I knelt, he announced to the class, "Kessler broke his computer! Oh, my *God!* He fried his shit!" And the class laughed, until Miss Rigg said, "Gus! Sit!" and he did, but not without laughing uncontrollably, and histrionically, as he staggered to his seat. "They'll never fix that jawn. It's in computer heaven! Oh. My. God!" he laughed.

Quickly, I shoved the pieces of the computer into my bottom drawer and resolved to let it remain there, unspoken of and forgotten until the day I retired, when I would say it was stolen. I glowered at Gus where he sat at his desk. He had laid his head down on his arm, pounding his knee with his fist, laughing delightedly—a picture of *schadenfreude*—so he missed the daggers that shot from my eyes. I retreated to lick my wounds.

In the English office, Mr. Wood was involved in a very bland sandwich: turkey and tomato on pumpernickel, something I might eat—on a weekend. He was sitting with a student advising him on how to proceed on a writing project, so I sat and ate a banana in silence. At the other end of the table stood the replica of a castle, which one of Mr. Hegel's students had created from a thousand popsicle sticks.

When Wood finished with his student, I asked, "What's this?"

"Tower of London, I think," said Wood. "Actually, it looks like the inner sanctum of the tower, the keep. The whole tower would be a Herculean task, even for one of Hegel's architects. It's complex. Ever seen it?"

"No, I've never been abroad," I said.

"You should go," said Wood, and I must have looked a bit flustered as I bit into my banana, because Wood looked me over and asked, "Everything OK?"

"Yes, fine," I said.

"Observed yet?"

"No, not yet."

"Got your grades ready?"

"All set."

The fragrance of lilacs announced the arrival of Worthington, who clicked in quickly, followed by three young ladies who were dressed for business. There was Kim, her friend Lorraine, and another young lady. "Guess what?" said Worthington as she sat, and her entourage stood together beaming, "Kim's going to Harvard."

Kim and her court squealed a celebratory squeal. "I can't believe it," Kim said breathlessly as she brandished a letter with the official letterhead of Harvard University.

"I can," said Wood, "Congratulations!"

"I guess they need girls," I said innocently enough, though it made the celebrations cease momentarily until Worthington changed the subject.

"Are you girls ready to meet the mayor?" she asked.

"All set. Should we show him the lunchroom? That place gets a little unruly sometimes."

"I don't see how you can avoid it if he wants to see it," said Worthington, and turning to us she said, "Mayor Nutter is visiting today, and the Ushers are showing him around."

"When's he coming?" I asked.

"Very soon," said Worthington, "You girls need to get going." Worthington shooed them, and they filed out with exuberant giggling.

Principal Hirshburg was outside the office, and he met the girls as they left. He told them how lovely they were and jocularly reminded them not to talk politics with the mayor unless they gave him praise. The girls complied with laughter. Then the principal entered the office and, after he acknowledged Worthington with a wave, he beckoned me into the hallway by curling his finger. My first thought was that someone had already told the boss about my killed computer. My colleagues watched me as I nervously followed the principal into the hall—Worthington knowingly, Wood confused—and, in the hall, the principal gave me the date and time for the next meeting with Latovick and his people. He told me I should get in touch with my union for representation, and his gravity was ominous. The date that he gave me was one day after the Observation Ms. Schlect had granted. Without consolation, Principal Hirshburg turned brusquely and walked off. There was a sharp pain in my upper back.

"What was that all about?" asked Wood when I returned.

I didn't know what to say. I thought of saying "Nothing," but Worthington knew all about it, so it seemed futile to evade the question. I was certainly close enough to Wood by this time that I could share a professional problem and maybe even seek some advice. Still, I was loath to explain. I twisted in my seat and stammered something like "I don't know."

"Should I tell him?" asked Worthington.

"Go ahead," I said.

She knew more about the case than I did. She explained how a parent accused me of cheating on a benchmark test by defining the word "fiasco" before the test (Wood laughed); she told how the District sent a "pit bull" named Latovick to prosecute me, and how, though the principal wanted the whole matter to disappear, the District wanted to make an example; then she went into some of the ancillary issues, like how Mrs. Hegel saw an opportunity to criticize the test by compiling a list of misleading and ambiguous questions she'd found on previous tests, and how my case was causing a stir among her fellow coordinators around the city. Worthington finished by explaining that Principal Hirshburg's cabinet saw the case as an attempt to humble the school because of its high profile and continuing success.

"Some kerfuffle," said Wood. "It's always a treat to deal with the folks downtown."

"What gets me," I said, "is I was talking to Mrs. Kessler about this, and she was telling me that cheating is rampant throughout the District. That teachers coach students *during* the test, not before it, and principals require teachers to alter the answer sheets..."

"Really?" Worthington said dryly.

"How is Mrs. Kessler?" asked Wood.

"Fine," I said.

"Why doesn't she bake cookies for us anymore?" asked Wood, referring to a time a few years ago when Mrs. Kessler inexplicably baked thousands of Christmas cookies and we had to find outlets for them. I'd brought a few hundred to school, and this was all Mr. Wood or anyone else at Northwest knew of Mrs. Kessler. I think Mrs. Kessler and I ate one cookie each.

"She quit the cookie business."

Wood was unimpressed with my cheating dilemma. If anything, he found it funny. "I think administrators get bored and need things to do," he said. "After all, what do they do all day? Dream up assembly programs? Walk the halls? Confer with the dietitian? What? Once at Peale I had the occasion to go downtown to the Administration office and I learned something very peculiar about administrators...."

Wood was beginning another story. I was taken unawares.

I peeked into my briefcase to see if I had my tape recorder and a tape spooled to the beginning. I had to eject the tape in the machine and insert a new tape, and I fumbled a bit with the record buttons. But I did all this inside my briefcase, so no one noticed. Worthington made herself comfortable with her salad, and I had an opportunity to forget my troubles for a while as Wood told us this tale. Once again, I have smoothed the prose a bit. He began:

When you go downtown to the Administration office, you always get a runaround. One secretary sends you to another secretary; that one sends you back to the first one; you wait for a spell, then you go somewhere else. You know how it is. But of all the runarounds I ever experienced doing business at the Administration office, the worst was the time Peale sent me to put some photographs away for safekeeping. Apparently these photographs were valuable, so the School District wanted to keep them downtown in their archives and, since I was the person in charge of photography for Peale, I took them downtown and, let me tell you, it took a whole day to search for an office that was willing to file these photographs—even though I had a specific room number to take them to—and, in the end, no one took them. In fact I still have them at home hanging on my wall. I think they're valuable...pictures of the Republican presidential candidate, Alf Landon, campaigning in the school's yard back in the '30s. Very nice.

Anyhow, I learned a valuable lesson from that trip to the Administration office, and it wasn't that you always get a runaround—everyone knows that—it was something deeper, something subtler.

First I went to the Office of Curriculum and Development because, for some reason, that was where my principal told me to go. The receptionist in that office sent me back to the secretary. The secretary sent me in to see the administrative assistant, and the administrative assistant sent me to the coordinator herself. She sent me along to the Supervisor of Curriculum and Development. And finally, the Supervisor allowed me to wait for the Curriculum and Development Leader, who wasn't there, but no matter; the Supervisor made the decision that their office was not in charge of storing photographs, and she showed me the door. She told me to try the Office of Art Education. There, the receptionist sent me to the secretary; the secretary sent me to the administrative assistant; she sent me to the coordinator, who sent me to the supervisor, and so forth, until I met the Art Leader, who was there, but she also told me that her office was not a place to store photos. She sent me to the Office of District Archives, way down in the basement. They too had a receptionist to greet me, a secretary to send me on to an administrative assistant, and a number of coordinators, deputies, and supervisors—all, as with my previous stops, in successive anterooms, deeper and deeper into an office suite, until at the end there was a leader, who rejected the photos and pointed me to a door that led into the hallway. District Archives sent me to another building, a few miles away, where the District stored paper and furniture and office supplies in a huge warehouse. This building worked exactly the same as the other building. A receptionist allowed me to enter a suite of offices, and successive bureaucrats allowed me to penetrate deeper into the suite until I met the leader, or the supervisor, or whatever top dog was making decisions that day, and she sent me packing. Finally, I went back to the original building, this time to the Office of Building Maintenance, and when I had completed the routine and climbed to the top of the totem of that office with no success, I decided to take the photographs back to my own school and store them in a shoe box in the closet in the back of my classroom, which was probably more safe than the District Office anyway, and that was where they stayed, until I transferred here and took the photos home.

But I'm trying to tell you the "valuable lesson" I learned from this bureaucratic shuffling, and the lesson was something truly bizarre. It was this: Every time I moved farther and farther into the inner recesses of one of those District offices, I noticed that the administrator was bigger and bigger in accordance with the importance of her position. I mean physically bigger. The receptionist was always petite. The secretary was about a size 6 or 8. The coordinator was at least a 10. And everyone above the level of coordinator did her shopping in the plus-size store. The leader was, in every case, a huge mountain of a woman. Moreover, the clothing of these women—they were all women— became more and more gown-like as I moved further into the vestibules of power. So the receptionist wore slacks and a blouse; the secretary wore a suit, the administrative assistant wore a fancy shift, the coordinator wore an ornate muumuu, and the

supervisor and the leader competed for the most expansive, the
most diaphanous, the most free-flowing robes they could find to
cover their impressive bulk. The leader was, without exception,
always the biggest woman of all. Some leaders were well over six
feet tall and more than three hundred pounds—very impressive
in their perfumed robes of pastel layers and exotic fabrics. The
leader was like a queen bee, sitting in the innermost office—the
best appointed office, with the most opulent furnishings and
most superfluous decorations—a very formidable officer, as
wide as a tent in her layers of robes, bedecked with silver and
shells and gold and stones (and did I see a few bones)—and, most
impressive, the leader, and only the leader, always wore a fine hat
to complement her gown. That was the peculiar but interesting
lesson that I learned that day—that my School District promoted
its personnel based on their physical size.

(Here Wood mentioned something about Worthington
being doomed to outer offices in her quest for administrative
advancement, on account of her slender frame.)

So, when we got a new principal at our school, I was not
surprised to see how big she was. Her position was not important
enough for her to wear a hat, but she was an impressive sight
nevertheless. She stood more than six feet tall. Her shoulders
were unusually broad, and her frame was very square. She
lacked all traces of a shape—she had no curves, but she wasn't
fat—just big and wide. And her legs were shaped like bowling
pins. Unlike her important colleagues downtown, Ms. Cole, the
new principal, did not wear those distinctive flowing robes.
Instead, she always wore a ladies' business suit, with buttons
down the front of her skirt, buttons down the front of her jacket,
and buttons down the front of her blouse. When my colleague,
Ms. Fortunata, first laid eyes on Ms. Cole, she remarked, "Look
at all those buttons! If I were that size, I wouldn't split myself in
two like that."

Ms. Fortunata had a talent for fashion—and criticism. It was
Ms. Fortunata who noticed that Ms. Cole's hairstyle was identical
to the hairstyle of Little Iodine, the comic book character from
the '50s. Cole had the distinctive Little Iodine bangs in front,
and the same tightly pulled bun in the back. She even had some
Iodinesque wisps of hair springing from above her forehead, and
she wore a bow in the middle of her head, just like Little Iodine. It

was as though she took an old Dell comic book to the hairdresser, just as someone might take a Glamour *magazine, and told the hairdresser she wanted to look like Little Iodine.*

After Ms. Fortunata's insightful observation about the hairstyle of Ms. Cole, I began to see in our principal more and more of a resemblance to the naughty comic book character from my childhood. Cole had the same round cheeks as Iodine, the same thin eyebrows, and the same round chin. Yes, Ms. Cole was the spittin' image of Little Iodine. Except for her big body. Her head, in fact, was entirely too small for her big body, so it seemed the actual head of Little Iodine had been screwed into the big body of our new principal. In casual conversation, Ms. Fortunata and I invariably referred to Ms. Cole as Little Iodine.

Early in the year, our peculiar new principal revealed the nature of her personality. We were about to begin the first department meeting of the year, when our colleague, Mitch McKid, walked into the meeting a little late and said, "Wu'zzuuuuuuh?" This "Wu'zzuuuuuuh" came from the popular beer commercial on TV at the time—the one where these black guys greet each other with hilarious modifications of "What's up?" In the commercial, one guy calls another guy on the phone and says, "Wu'zzuuuuuuh?" and the other guy answers back, "Wu'zzuuuuuuh?" and then they explain to each other that they are just sitting around "watching the game, drinking a Bud." A few other guys call, there are a few more "Wu'zzuuuuuuh's?" And the commercial is funny because of the distinctive way each character intones his "Wu'zzuuuuuuh?" They say it with such a slow, drawn-out disdain for formality—"Wu'zzuuuuuuh?" Anyhow, Mitch McKid had his own distinctive "Wu'zzuuuuuuh?" down pat. He walked into the department meeting late and performed it for the whole department. Everyone cracked up. Then Mr. Bean, to show he also was hip, answered McKid's "Wu'zzuuuuuuh?" with a very thin "Wu'zzuuuuuuh?" So McKid said, "No, like this," and he demonstrated his "Wu'zzuuuuuuh?" Mr. Bean tried it again. This time Bean's "Wu'zzuuuuuuh?" was a little better, though he needed practice, and this prompted Ms. Jenks, our department head, to demonstrate a "Wu'zzuuuuuuh?" for him, and hers was pretty good, for a girl. Then everyone started trying it.

"Wu'zzuuuuuuh?"

"Wu'zzuuuuuuh?"

"Wu'zzuuuuuuh?"

And we were practicing this silly expression, with varying degrees of success, until the whole room rang with the phrase, and we sounded like a barnyard or a modernist symphony orchestra, with a cacophony of "Wu'zzuuuuuuh's?" resounding all around the room, and a lot of laughter in between.

Just then the formidable presence of our new principal, Ms. Cole, filled the doorway, and our crazy "Wu'zzuuuuuuh's?" trailed off. Unfortunately, Mr. McKid, who had led the "Wu'zzuuuuuuh?" frenzy, was too caught up in the moment, and he turned to the door where Cole stood and voiced his very best "Wu'zzuuuuuuh?" for her, complete with the grotesque facial distortion that this phrase engendered. Cole was not amused. Her Iodine eyebrows raised and her thin lips pursed. She used her index finger to signal Ms. Jenks into the hallway. We could hear our new principal reaming Ms. Jenks in the hallway, and she wasn't quiet about it, telling her to get her "people" in order or she'd get them in order for her and that making "obscene" noises was not part of the agenda she'd prescribed. Jenks returned chastened, and this was how we learned that ol' Ms. Cole was not a merry old soul.

Cole decreed that she would evaluate every teacher in the school based on the results of a standardized test—I forget which test was popular at the time—and she would deem any teacher whose students did not measure up to certain standards as unsatisfactory. Once a teacher was labeled "unsatisfactory," he or she would need remediation, and this remediation would consist of her personally observing the teacher and making recommendations. Failure to comply with these recommendations would result in further remediation, further Observation, yet more recommendations, and finally reassignment. That's right: You'd get thrown out.

Naturally, we hated her. Students at Peale were not the kind of students who did well on standardized tests, so ninety percent of the teachers in the school were rated "unsatisfactory." Only the few teachers who taught the few accelerated classes managed to slip through her selection process.

For months, we saw ol' Ms. Cole trudging stiffly through

the hallways on her bowling pin legs, clutching her infernal clipboard, on her way to evaluate and demean her next victim. She lumbered along with that pinched expression on her little face, and she sat in the back of each teacher's class for the entire excruciating class period. Her Observations were completely negative, and often she was cruel. I never heard her utter a word of praise.

Big ol' Cole sat in the back of my class one morning, towering over the largest students in the twelfth grade, hardly fitting in a student chair, scribbling her poisonous observations on her clipboard and scowling as she scanned my room looking for objectionable items. I stood in front of the class, teaching my lesson and thinking my observer looked like a Little Iodine balloon that Macy's might float through the air on Thanksgiving Day—so huge was she in her many-buttoned suit and so Iodine-like from the neck up. I was rated as "conditionally satisfactory," pending the next examination, though Ms. Cole found plenty of room for improvement in my performance which I, like everyone else, took personally. To read one of Ms. Cole's Observations was to become emotionally upset. She had a real knack for denigrating people. Ms. Fortunata's assessment of the situation was astute, as usual, though understated. "Our new principal is not a people person," she said.

Students learned to dislike the principal too. She brought more and more standardized tests into the school, she said, to "raise standards." Some of the tests were very hard, and there was a new battery of tests every month, giving many students the opportunity to fail a test on a regular basis. Students dreaded these tests and complained bitterly. There was real tension in the school at one point. Students were going to stage a protest demonstration; there were letters from parents, and a feeling of unrest pervaded the school.

To placate the students before a particularly grueling battery of tests, the principal allowed, at one point, a special assembly program called "The Test Relief Concert"—which featured a rap singer named Dead Lee. His rap tunes were distinguished by their "positive values." Dead Lee did not offend adults with subversive lyrics. He rapped about ending violence, and he rapped about the evils of drugs, and he supported the police with a tune entitled "The Cops Is Da Man." I even heard Dead Lee rap *some very compelling lyrics about the benefits of brushing one's teeth regularly. On the morning of the concert, the students in the audience were having a ball listening to Dead Lee. They were out of their seats dancing and waving their arms around. I thought this assembly might smooth the friction between the principal and the students over the issue of testing. But disaster struck. Mr. Dead Lee performed a composition called "No Mo' Babies," which eschewed teenage pregnancy, and this composition contained the word "damn," which prompted Principal Cole to come forward and personally stop the show. Cole emerged from the wings of the stage, where she seemed to have positioned herself for an ambush, seconds after "damn" was uttered, frightening Dead Lee. His eyes widened as Cole approached him, and he saw her tremendous bulk and her angry demeanor. She swiped his microphone and ordered the house lights turned up, splashing cold water on the dancing students.*

"Stop having fun!" she ordered, pointing at the stunned audience. An angry murmur rolled through the auditorium, and the principal stared down the crowd with her orneriest Little Iodine stare. An undertone of anger arose. Suddenly, from somewhere in the crowd, someone hurled a pint carton of orange juice at the principal. It was no lob either, but a hard pitch, thrown like a line drive, right at the shoulder of Ms. Cole, and it was a direct hit—it hit Ms. Cole squarely above her left breast. Remarkably, the carton, which was full, bounced off Cole's chest like a ping-pong ball, and her super-human strength surprised everyone into silence. She didn't even flinch when she was hit. The students, though not very happy, were impressed, and they settled down. The principal dismissed the assembly, and she excused Mr. Dead Lee from any further school engagements.

This incident erased any last traces of popularity Ms. Cole might have had among students. They dubbed her "Oddjob" for her imperviousness to missiles and her cold, unemotional nature.

Just before Christmas, Ms. Cole enacted a piece of legislation that the staff found unforgivable. She cut everyone's overtime pay in half. She said that unless test scores rose, she would ultimately disband all extracurricular activities, but in the meantime she required every teacher who had an extracurricular activity to cut the activity time in half and settle for half the pay. For those of us who did extra work after school, this act was even more insulting than the harsh observations—this was money!

Ms. Fortunata was one of the hardest hit by the cuts. She was the sponsor of the school's yearbook, a mammoth task, and for her to do her job in half the time at half the salary was unthinkable. I worked with Ms. Fortunata from time to time in my capacity as school photographer, and I noticed she was descending into a real funk about this overtime issue. She grew unusually quiet and sullen, and when she did speak she was curt and testy. I found I couldn't say a word to her that she didn't find annoying. Fortunata was a moody woman, and when she was in a dark mood you didn't want to get too close to her. Depressed, she was like a hungry alligator submerged in a pool of misery, and she was just looking for some unsuspecting soul to come near her pond, so she could rear up and snap off his head.

I had just taken some pictures of the Charm Club, an activity designed to smooth some of the rough edges off our young ladies, and I brought these pictures to Ms. Fortunata

She did not look up from her computer when I came into her room.

"Pictures of the Charm Club," I announced, placing the pictures on Ms. Fortunata's desk.

She rolled her eyes and peered at me above her half-glasses. Looking impatient, she reluctantly picked up the pictures and flipped through them in a second. "They stink!"

"But there are plenty to choose from—"

"You jerk!" Fortunata exploded, "How many times have I told you not to waste a lot of film on a stupid activity."

"But—"

"But me no buts! You know, you're a real piece of work. You go out and snap a few pictures and you actually get paid for it! It's amazing. Some people do the stupidest things, and they make the same money as I do! And I have a real job! Do you realize what it takes to make this book? It's hard. It's grueling. It's thankless! What the hell is the Charm Club anyway? Do they wear little white gloves and drink tea in the afternoon? Do they walk around with books balanced on their heads? What? What's going on around here? Do you honestly think I'm going to make a yearbook for half the money. I... I... I..." Fortunata was getting pretty worked up. She'd mussed her hair. She'd tossed a few of my pictures around the room. And she'd knocked over a little *trophy she'd once received for being Teacher of the Year.*

"Calm down, Kay," I said, "everyone has lost money..."

Kay picked up her trophy and stared at it. Before I could finish what I was saying, she began to shudder, and then she began to sob, and then she burst out crying. She fell into her chair with her face in her hands and wailed.

I'd never seen her cry before. I thought she was pretty hard-boiled. "Kay, what's the matter?" I asked. She couldn't be crying just because she'd lost some overtime pay. "What's up?"

"I can't tell you."

"Can't tell me? What are you talking about? Is it trouble at home?"

"No."

"It's that big old principal, isn't it?" I pulled up a chair and sat next to my colleague to commiserate.

"Yes," whimpered Kay.

"What is it this time? Did she observe you again?"

"No. Not that. It's too weird to tell," Kay wiped her eyes, trying to fix her mascara.

"Weird? She is kind of weird, isn't she, with that little head and that huge body. Did I ever tell you my theory about how they promote women down at the District? It's based on their size?" I was about to tell Ms. Fortunata about the time I tried to get the pictures filed and met the big, giant leaders, but before I could begin, Kay interrupted.

"She's not big," said Kay.

"Not big? Who's not big?

"The principal."

"Oh, she's big," I said. "She's enormous. Didja' ever look at her tits? It's like she's carrying a keg—"

"No," said Kay. "She's not big. She's tiny."

"Well, I know her head is tiny. She looks like Little Io—"

"Shut up and listen," said Kay, regaining her composure, taking her compact from her bag. "Listen to me. I want to tell you something... Remember that meeting we had with the principal in her conference room, when she told us she was cutting our overtime?"

"Yes."

"Do you remember when the meeting was over, when we were leaving, how I had to go to the bathroom, and I went

back into the principal's conference room and used her private bathroom?"

"Yes, I remember. I told you not to do that. Big shots don't like it when you use—"

Kay grabbed my lapel and shook to shut me up. She looked at me seriously with her smeary eyes. "Will you please just listen!" she ordered. I piped down and she continued. "When I opened the door to the principal's powder room, she was sitting on the pot."

"Oh, my God, you caught the principal peeing?"

"Yes, but that's not important. What's important is that she was—she was—tiny. Teeny-tiny. Her big body is just a big suit she wears."

"Huh? Tiny? A suit?"

"Yes, it's a suit! When I surprised her on the potty she was sitting there in just a bra, with her bloomers around her ankles, and she was as small as a ten-year-old girl. Her feet didn't even touch the floor. Next to her, leaning on the sink, were her clothes—like a big suit of armor or a big life jacket. It's her clothes that make her look big." Kay grabbed both of my lapels this time, and she shook me to make me understand. "Do you get it? Cole puts on a big, puffed-up suit to make her look big. It buttons up the front, and it is filled with—something—some kind of stuffing, maybe Styrofoam." Kay shook me harder, knocking my glasses awry. "Do you understand me? On the other side of the bathroom were her legs. They're like stilts, or prosthetic legs—that she stands on.... She walks on stilts!" Kay let go of my jacket. "You don't believe me."

"Yes," I said. "I do believe you." It was an incredible story, but it did explain some things, like why Principal Cole walked so stiffly, and why things bounced off her, and why her clothing had so many buttons and, most of all, why her head was so small.

Kay summed things up. "Sitting on the toilet, without her big suit and her stilts, she looked just like—"

We said it together, "Little Iodine!"

I prepared some tea, and we had a discussion, and before long Ms. Fortunata and I were having a good laugh about the principal's charade. I explained to Kay how necessary it was for Ms. Cole to be a big woman in the District if she wanted to be promoted, and Kay believed me. She was in a mood to believe anything. I could have told her that one must speak Albanian to get a promotion in our District and she would have believed me. That would make as much sense as dressing in a costume every day to appear bigger than you are. What was troubling Kay was that the principal might seek some kind of revenge because Kay knew too much. When I asked Kay what she planned to do, she was quick to respond. "I want you to take a picture of Ms. Cole without her suit," said Kay. "I'd feel better if I had some proof of what I saw."

I don't know why I accepted this assignment from Ms. Fortunata. It was a dangerous assignment—photographing Ms. Cole without her suit. Perhaps I accepted the assignment because Ms. Fortunata and I had been colleagues and friends for so many years. Perhaps I accepted because it was a photographic challenge. Perhaps I accepted the assignment because I always accepted Kay's assignments. She'd sent me all around the city where our students were singing, or helping people, or making speeches; she'd sent me on seven-mile treks to photograph students walking to benefit AIDS charities; she sent me on class trips out of town where I had to get up at four in the morning and didn't get back until twelve at night. I always brought back the pictures. I am pretty sure of one thing: I accepted the assignment because I wanted to see Ms. Cole in her true state—a little woman wearing a big suit—and I wanted to see this for myself, regardless of the consequences.

We conceived the following plan: I would sneak up to the home of Ms. Cole in the evening when she was likely to be relaxing without her costume, and I would peep into a window of her home with my camera and get a shot of her without her business suit. Kay knew where Ms. Cole lived. She lived in a swanky suburb where all the streets were named after English earls, like Sussex and Trent. Cole lived at 16 Northumberland Road in a spacious Tudor-style home. I decided to bring a little old rangefinder camera I sometimes used, very quiet to operate, and visit her that very night.

I parked a few blocks away from 16 Northumberland, down a winding road in a cul-de-sac. With camera in hand, I approached Ms. Cole's mansion. Her gardener was just finishing spraying the trees on her property with a noisy industrial-strength sprayer that was attached to a water truck; I think he *was washing the trees. I waited for him to finish, and when he did, he wound his hose onto the water truck and pulled away, leaving the neighborhood to descend quietly into twilight.*

I looked up the long sward of grass that led to Cole Manor, and I saw one lone light burning in a window on the second floor. The first floor of the house—it appeared to me—was devoted to the garage, and Ms. Cole lived on the upper floors. I would have to climb a tree to do my spying. I looked for the likeliest tree.

There was a huge copper beech on the property, whose branches would give access to the illuminated window, but it would require quite a climb. The trunk of the tree was short and squat, but each of its lower branches stretched thirty feet, rising at a gentle slope, and one of these branches ended near the lighted window. I might get a peek in the window if I shimmied to the end of the branch.

I shouldered my camera and started to climb. I climbed the trunk of the tree easily. Then I hugged the long limb that led to the window. I had to scale it like a koala. I inched along on my chest. It bobbed and creaked as I crawled.

I put all thoughts about the trouble I'd be in if I got caught out of my mind. Instead, to amuse myself, I wondered if, like Ms. Cole herself, her big house was not a big house at all but a little bungalow with a big house wrapped around it. Perhaps her big Town Car, which was parked in the driveway, was not a big Town Car at all but a small Plymouth Horizon with a Town Car shell; perhaps this big tree was just a little dogwood; and—oh my God—perhaps the enormous Rottweiler that had appeared beneath the tree was only a tiny Pomeranian in disguise.

Yes, a big dog, unleashed and appearing out of nowhere, looked curiously up at me as I climbed toward the lit window. He cocked his head and stared, as if to say, "I am certain that you will fall soon; so I will wait here a moment until you do, and then I will eat you." Although I didn't like being treed by Ms. Cole's watchdog, I thanked God he did not bark. How could I explain this situation? "Oh, hi Ms. Cole, I just thought I'd drop by and check the job the gardener did on the tree.

It was growing darker by the moment, and the inquisitive dog blended into the night. I had no choice but to continue upward and worry about Hans, or whatever his name was, when the time came. As long as he didn't bark.

I crawled farther up the branch.

However, when I was just beneath the window, Hansie became alarmed and started barking a warning. I immediately heard footsteps approach the window, not six feet away from me. The window flew open, and a woman with red hair, wearing the uniform of a Victorian domestic, emerged and looked down at the dog. I clutched the tree tightly. I felt the urge to pee. "What is it, Hans?" the woman asked. (How had I known the dog's name?) She looked all around, including right at me, as the dog barked urgently. But she couldn't see me in the darkness. I looked like a part of the tree, obscured by leaves and twisting branches. Hans made one more desperate bark—"He's right beneath you," Hans's bark said. "Quiet, Hans!" said the woman. "Chase your rabbits quietly!" She closed the window and padded back into the room. Hans shut up.

With Hans's doggie eyes following me, I came to the top of the branch. I could go no farther. If Ms. Cole were not in this room, Ms. Fortunata would have to do without these pictures. I certainly wasn't going to pull another stunt like this. My back was aching; my hands were shredded; my thighs were chafed; and Hans was surely very angry with me for any embarrassment I had caused him.

I pulled up to the height of the window—and there it was. I couldn't have asked for a more perfect tableau. Ms. Cole, in profile, sat at her dining table, clear as could be. She was teeny-tiny; her little feet dangled above the floor. Across from her sat her husband, reading the newspaper. The servant in the uniform was placing a big bowl of potato chips between them on the table. Cole's husband was a small chap, but Cole herself, in a little terry bathrobe, was child-sized. She clapped her hands, saying, "Oh goodie goodie!" as the bowl of chips landed on the table.

I took my camera off my shoulder and shot picture after picture through the window. I shot a whole roll of good clear pictures. There was enough light in the room so I didn't need a strobe. The whole scene was about ten feet from me, so the composition was easy. Best of all, the big, solid furnishings in the room—the heavy sideboard and the grand breakfront, not to mention the good-sized servant—made ol' Ms. Cole look oh-so-small and made the pictures very funny. These pictures would be good. Tomorrow everyone in the school would know the truth about their troublesome principal. When I finished, I rested a minute and started down.

Climbing down was harder than climbing up because I climbed backward and I couldn't see what was behind me. I kept bumping into nubs and branches. This unnerved me, and I jumped off the branch onto the ground a little sooner than I should have and twisted my ankle. I expected to confront Hans when I landed, but he was nowhere in sight. Exhausted, I sat at the base of the tree to catch my breath and thought, "Won't Ms. Fortunata get a kick out of these pictures!" But when I hoisted myself up to go, Hans emerged from the darkness. He must have been hiding, waiting for his moment to pounce.

I said, "Nice Hansie," and tried to walk past him, but he growled and blocked my path. I tried another path, but he growled and blocked me again. He had a really menacing growl. I noticed his eyes followed my camera wherever it moved. I thought, "Maybe he wants to play." I took a quarter from my pocket and threw it, hoping he would chase it, but his eyes stayed fixed on the camera. I bent down gingerly and picked up a twig and tossed it, but Hans kept his eyes on the camera. I made like I was going to throw the camera, and Hans flinched. "Uh oh," I thought, "The camera is my price for freedom." I tried putting the camera in my back pocket, but Hans bared his teeth and growled until I showed him the camera. I knew that if I threw the camera, Hans would chase it, and I would be able to limp away, but this would mean losing a favorite camera, along with the great shots of Little Iodine in her bathrobe.

Instead, I attempted to flee, and this made Hans lose all patience. He sprang forward and bit me. He bit me hard on the back of my leg, then jumped up and bit my arm. Then he ran in front of me and barked and snapped until I stopped. "OK," I said, "You win. You can have the damned camera." I gave him the camera, and I limped away. Hans had bitten the same leg of the ankle I'd twisted. As I disappeared into the darkness, Hans called, "Woof, woof!" after me, which I distinctly heard as "Thank you" in Rottweiler. And I cursed myself for not thinking of extracting the film from the camera before I sacrificed it.

Because I bore wounds, Ms. Fortunata was not disappointed the next day when I showed up without the film. She was so amused by my story, she didn't even care about the pictures. She especially liked the part of the story where the dog bit me; it made her howl with laughter. And she loved the part that happened after Hans bit me and I couldn't find my car. I wandered around the suburbs bleeding for an hour, looking at street signs with the names of English nobility, until I found my car and drove myself to the hospital.

"Poor little you," said Fortunata, having a fine laugh and inspecting my bandaged arm.

As for Ms. Cole's secret, it turned out it was no secret at all. Lots of people knew she was a little person wearing a big suit. It was just no one wanted to say anything because everyone was afraid. She was capable of anything. The only person I ever heard say anything about Ms. Cole's secret was a profoundly retarded student. He waited for a quiet moment during an assembly program when Ms. Cole was making a speech about the school's new spate of testing. Between statements, when the audience was hushed, the intellectually challenged kid said, "Her head's too small for her body." Everybody heard this, and I swore that everyone in the whole auditorium could clearly see that ol' Ms. Cole was wearing a big suit just then, but nobody said anything....

A pause ensued.

"Did your principal ever come clean?" I asked.

Worthington seemed surprised at my credulity.

"Never," said Wood. "The superintendent promoted her to a job downtown and she left after only a few years."

"Who replaced her?" asked Worthington. "Pee-Wee Herman?"

"Oh, the next guy was even more incredible," said Wood. "No lie."

Another story on tape, I thought, *and this one more incredible than the others.* If Wood kept this up, I'd have enough material to write a whole book when I retired.

11. The part that's hardest to tell

BY EAVESDROPPING on Wood's class for a few days during my preparation period, pretending to use the heat register outside his door as a shelf to rest my briefcase while I organized it, I ascertained his method of teaching symbolism in Kafka. What he did, essentially, was slow down and assume his students knew nothing. He spent a whole period demonstrating what symbolism is. I would normally define symbolism in three minutes, just mentioning that a symbol is something that stands for something else. Not Wood. He gave a definition, which students copied (I could do that). Then he read a parable by James Thurber, something about a duck with two mouths and one ear (I could do that). There was a discussion about symbolism in the Thurber story (I could try that). Then he had pairs of students analyze some surrealist paintings he projected on a screen (I couldn't do that; that would take a projector and a background in art history that I didn't have). He was about to distribute copies of a story he himself had written when I'd had enough and decided I could extrapolate a lesson from what I'd seen and come up with something that would satisfy Frau Schlect.

I had always taken for granted that students knew what symbolism is by the time they were in the twelfth grade, but I could see how it was unwise to take anything for granted when it came to kids. So I set about creating my own lesson on symbolism that would consume a whole period, and I would keep this lesson ready for my appointment with Ms. Schlect. When she came, my students would consider the issue of the bug as a symbol, and it would fit right in.

To speak truth, when Wood was standing before his students, preparing to distribute his homemade story, and his class was about to rearrange their seats and separate into groups (a modern educational trend I despise), where they would analyze his story, I was seized with another attack of jealousy, and that was part of the reason I stopped watching. Specifically, just before Wood's students repaired into groups, there was a short discussion between Wood and Lorraine, one of Kim's gang of future Ivy Leaguers, and it was an insight of Lorraine's that made me cringe with a palpable feeling of jealousy. "There's such a feeling of helplessness in this story," Lorraine said, "because Gregor is not responsible for his transformation. He's like Oedipus—up against evil beyond his control. I mean, he didn't choose to be a bug. So it's kind of like evil is the natural way of the world and Gregor is a victim...." Wood was about to field Lorraine's comment when I fled, thinking how I had never in my entire career elicited such a comment from a student.

I have tried to think of a way not to tell this next part of the story because it's so hard to tell. I admired Worthington, and I hated to lose her friendship. She always knew what was afoot in the school and when to be cautious. Though she was young, she brought to our lunch group a kind of mature sensibility, looking astonished at Wood or me when we behaved questionably. She was attached to the school's administration and, therefore, she was a beneficial ally, especially in my trouble with the testing people, where her position as testing coordinator made her an invaluable friend. Consequently, the next problem that I encountered affected me most inasmuch as it caused a breach between Worthington and me. It also was the most direct reason for my deciding to retire, so I don't see how I can avoid the telling, though I'd like to.

A day or two after I broke my computer, I was sitting in the English office during lunch, munching on an apple and using Mrs. Hegel's computer to enter my students' grades for the quarter. Hegel was across the hall teaching and my laptop was interred in my bottom drawer. Although I was making the grades up off the top of my head—being more than generous—I was pretending to be copying them from a spreadsheet, which was actually a hard copy of a previous set of grades. This pretense of copying from a hard copy—making it look like I had authentic grades—was for the sake of Worthington, who was sitting at the worktable sweating over a stack of essays she needed to correct in time for them to count in the current quarter. I thought, *Bad timing, Worthington. Giving essays close to the end of a quarter. Giving essays at all! Such a silly girl.* She was really bearing down on those papers, and I could see that Worthington would be working on her grades well into the night, while I was sipping a much-needed martini and watching the detectives on TV. Wood had left his lunch sitting on the table and gone to check a student's attendance in the roll books in the office. As we worked to meet the deadline for grades, there was an industrious silence in the office.

Into the room breezed my friend Augustus Merriwether. Neither our silence nor our industry deterred him from interrupting. "Hey," he called, seeing Mrs. Worthington and pulling at the back of his jeans to cover his shorts, "Y'all got a printer in here?"

"Augustus," said Worthington, "is that the way you enter a room and request a favor?"

"A'ight," he corrected himself, "May I *please* use the printer?" He brandished a small flash drive in the hand that was not holding up his pants.

"Why don't you use the library?" asked Worthington.

"Theirs ain't *workin'*. And besides, the librarian is evil. I think she's possessed. When she sees me, she bugs out!" Gus was in high spirits. He had shoved his baseball cap into his back pocket, ready to don it as soon as no authority was looking.

"What are you printing?" asked Worthington, hardly looking up from her task.

"An essay for Miss Rigg. I have it on this thing." He extended the little disk drive toward Worthington. "It's already a day late and she's threatening not to take it. You know she's crazy, right?"

"I know *you're* crazy." Worthington pointed Gus toward me, since I was seated at the computer.

Gus approached me, jabbing the drive in my direction as a request to insert it into the computer. He flashed an amused smile in my direction. "That's ma bro'! Broke his computer; jawn went down, and he felt like a clown." Gus teased. Worthington looked up with an expression that said it was inappropriate for me not to respond to this level of insubordination.

"Just give me the drive," I said.

"I guess Miss Rigg put you uptight," Gus confided softly. "She do be bringing it, wit' dem tight skirts, n'aw mean?" Gus clicked his cheek and winked.

It was then that I noticed that the drive that Gus had handed me was the one that had gone missing from my desk. I had marked it with a number one—"1"—with a Sharpie to distinguish it from another flash drive. Gus was handing me my stolen drive— indisputably marked. It could be no other. The full weight of this struck me like a sock in the jaw. Gus was the sneak thief who had been haunting me for months. I had suspected as much. I took the little device and said, "Hey, this is my drive."

Worthington looked up again.

Gus went on the offensive. "What is you talkin' about, your drive? That's mines. Oh, my *God!* I bought it a week ago. I can show you the receipt."

"No," I said, "look at the number one here. That's my number one." I rose from the computer.

Instinctively, Gus feinted and pulled back. He bit his lip. "Oh, my *God!* That's *my* number one. I wrote it on there because I have three of these. Oh, my God!" He turned to Mrs. Worthington, who was confused, "Why do y'all hire crazy people? This man is crazy. Miss Rigg had to curse him out the other day. He's upset because he dropped his computer. Next he'll say I broke his computer. He's lying on me!"

"Give me the drive," I said. "You will hear about this from the disciplinarian."

"Man," said Gus, "you can't prove this belongs to you. The only stuff on it is my stuff. Do you really think the disciplinarian scares me? You be buggin'. The disciplinarian and me is like this." Gus twisted his index and third fingers together. "Now getcha ass up and lemme use that printer. You can't lie on me."

Worthington was appalled, but deferred to me as the teacher in charge of this situation.

Now, I should have put the drive in my pocket—since I had it in my hand—and I should have walked Gus to the disciplinarian so a third party could sort this thing out. But this is easy to say now. Instead, I don't know exactly why, I continued to argue with Gus, "You're the liar," I said with some heat. "You lie with every breath. I've caught you lying red-handed—any number of times—and you know it."

"Man," said Gus, "you the liar. Who you told about that computer you hidin' in your drawer, huh?"

"Stick to the point," I sputtered. "This is my drive, and it's only one of a score of things you've stolen. You've been taking things out of my room all year!" Gus did a double-take at this and looked dumbstruck as I continued. "I don't think you can tell the truth from a lie. You don't know how to act in a class. That's why you get thrown out. You don't know how to act in the library. That's why the librarian gets sore at you. You don't know how to act in here. You've proven that. You don't know how to act at all. You don't know...*anything!*"

By this time I had worked myself into a rage. There was, of course, a lot going on in my life, a lot of stress, you might say, and I might have been a bit foggy from the extra drinking I'd been doing, and there were all those deadlines and meetings coming up and, well, I can admit now that it felt good to unload on Gus, and the angrier I got the better I felt. So I let it go. I pointed my finger in Gus's face and said, "Miss Rigg is right. You don't belong in this school. You're not fit for this school. Or any school. You're a liar and a thief!" I held up the evidence, the drive. "That's right, you're a thief. Fit more for prison than school. You belong in prison. Nothing but a dirty little thief who's been hounding me all year. Y'know what? You need to be put out of this school! You need to go back to the ghetto where you belong! Where everyone's a thief. Because I'll tell you what, you're nothing but a *nigger!*"

Worthington's eyes widened, and she rose.

Gus pointed his finger back at me and screeched, "You called me a nigger! You called me a nigger! I'll kick your ass, you faggot; you called me a n— You're fired!" and I think he was about to strike me, but Worthington put her arms around his waist, restraining him, and she drew him away from me and toward the door.

"Come on, Gus," she said, "you need to cool off in the office. Let's get this straightened out the right way." And she led the belligerent Gus out into the hall, where he could be heard accusing loudly, "He called me a nigger! That bug-faced, bald-headed, old asswipe called me a nigger," just as Mr. Wood reentered.

I stood near the computer, pallid and shaken, with the flash drive in my hand as though Gus had just returned it after a friendly loan, and Wood asked, "You used the n-word?"

I thought perhaps I could extenuate the circumstance by claiming to Wood that I'd said "Negro" instead of the n-word, but that was futile. It would all come out. There was a witness. "Yes," I said.

"Are you crazy?" asked Wood.

"Yes," I said, and I could still hear Gus shrieking the end of my career down the hall. I didn't care too much about that, though. All I wanted to do was apologize to Worthington and to un-say the word I'd said.

Mrs. Hegel, having heard the commotion, left her class and entered the office, "What's going on?" she said.

Wood, preparing to unwrap a sandwich of some sort, angled his thumb toward me and said, "Kessler used the n-word."

Mrs. Hegel was speechless.

12. More of the hard part

SOME exigencies cannot be avoided. Come what come may, fuel must be gathered, the baby must be fed, and the roof must be fixed. Just so, for a teacher, when grades are due, though other eventualities might stand in the way, grades must be entered—on time. After Worthington escorted Gus to the office, though my mind was distracted by the consequences to a point where my heart beat irregularly at least one time per minute, I sat back down at Mrs. Hegel's computer and continued to enter my students' grades until I was finished. The data might be spurious, the product of sheer conjecture on my part, but it was finished.

Wood also, constrained by the deadline, sat before his laptop at the worktable, calculating his students' grades.

"Where's your laptop?" he asked.

"I left it at home," I said.

Toward the end of the period, Worthington returned with Kim and Lorraine in tow. Worthington sat at the worktable and hastily took her salad from her bag, as though she couldn't afford the time she was using for lunch. The girls stood at the door looking sheepish. "Go ahead, ladies, tell him," said Worthington.

Wood and I looked up.

Kim spoke, "Mr. Kessler, we took the things from your room."

Worthington, crunching a vegetable, nodded at the disbelieving Wood.

"What...how?" I asked. I did not have the moral high ground from which to show anger.

Kim continued, "Mrs. Worthington gave us keys to her room so we could work after school, and the keys worked in your door. We snuck in your room after school and took your things. It was just a joke. We didn't mean any harm."

"But why would you take things from *me*?" I asked.

Lorraine answered this, "You seemed like the kind of teacher it would be fun to play with." Kim elbowed Lorraine gently, the Harvard student and the Kafka expert reduced to children.

"So how did Gus get my flash drive?"

"We gave it to him," said Kim. "He needed a drive and we let him use it."

Worthington dismissed the girls saying she would take care of this matter with them after school, and she continued with her salad, but not before she cut her eyes at me without speaking.

"Well," said Wood to Worthington, "how did all this come about?"

Worthington explained coolly, "The whole story came out in the Discipline Office. Gus told us about borrowing the drive from the girls and I investigated. I rounded up Kim and Lorraine and they cooperated. As for Mr. Kessler, and what he said, I explained the matter to everyone exactly as I witnessed it," Worthington ate with exaggerated calm. "Gus made such a fuss that he drew a pretty big crowd, including the principal. And I went ahead and told them everything."

"And?" asked Wood.

"And I don't know," Worthington said.

"I got so angry it slipped out," I said. "I didn't mean it."

Worthington hesitated as though she weren't going to answer this, but she did. She set down her fork and thought for a moment and said, "No, you did mean it. When you use that word you are not expressing anger, or talking to an individual; you are expressing a political position. You are making a sociological statement. You are coming to a conclusion you have drawn based on your experience and your attitude. To me, nothing sums up the basis of someone's thinking better than when they 'slip' with that word. I know Gus's mother. She's a bus driver. She won't be happy."

"But—" I stammered.

Worthington raised her palm. "Stop, Mr. Kessler. How long

have you been a teacher?"
"Thirty-nine and a half years."
"And you haven't learned anything yet?"
I couldn't defend myself. "Can *you* forgive me at least?"
"I don't think so."

13. Exile and anticlimax

THAT afternoon I submitted to the School District of Philadelphia a short, formal letter declaring my intention to retire at the end of the school year. As I have said, I had enough years in the system to assure a sufficient pension and, though it would have boosted my retirement pay by (exactly) four thousand forty dollars per year if I waited three years until the end of the contract, it didn't seem worth the daily emotional upset I was enduring. So I started the retirement ball rolling.

While I was signing in one morning soon after I sent my letter of intent, the principal beckoned me into his office for a chat. We did not sit. Holding a cup of coffee in one hand and placing his other hand on my shoulder, he looked me in the eye and said, without reservation or hesitation, "Mr. Kessler, it would be a good time for you to retire," and he smiled at me expectantly. In that smile I could see that he had not gotten the word from the District yet that I did intend to retire, but he had gotten word from Ms. Schlect that I was incompetent, and he had heard from Mrs. Worthington that I was a racist, and perhaps from Miss Rigg that I was a jerk, and of course he knew from Mr. Latovick that I was a cheat. I answered the principal, "The letter of my intention to separate from the School District is already in the mail." To which he said, quite earnestly, taking his hand from my shoulder, "Good. Because if you decide to stay, I have asked Mrs. Hegel to give you the absolute worst roster she can manage. Do we understand each other?"

And I said, "Yes, sir."

I could no longer face Mrs. Worthington, so I stopped going to the English office for lunch. Instead, when Miss Rigg displaced me during third period, I holed myself up in a small storage closet underneath the stairs in the library. Mrs. Diaz, the librarian, was kind enough to allow me this space, which was very well lit by a large fluorescent light above an old wooden students' desk where I ate lunch. I shared this closet with the books the library planned to discard and some old computer equipment, including an ancient Macintosh SE computer, shaped like a big brick, which actually worked when I plugged it in. At home, I found the grading program that I had used with a similar Mac back in the late eighties, and it worked. I spent my lunch period entering attendance and grades into this antique Mac, which actually required me to keep all my data and the grading application on three-and-a-quarter inch floppies—and swap these floppies every few minutes—since there was only enough space on the internal hard drive to run the operating system. I liked the old Mac. It reminded me of the Volkswagen in the Woody Allen movie that starts right up and runs after a few hundred idle years. Alone in this tiny insulated cell of a closet, munching a snack bar, surrounded by obsolete books, gazing into the nine-inch black and white screen of the old Mac, I avoided Mrs. Worthington and everyone else.

For two weeks, I was in a state of near-catatonic worry, thinking about the three appointments that awaited me: the meeting for cheating with Mr. Latovick, the meeting for name-calling with Mrs. Merriwether (Gus's mom), and the make-up Observation that Ms. Schlect had scheduled. Thinking about these meetings precipitated almost daily esophageal cramps, until I made an appointment with my doctor. He diagnosed my symptoms as a stomach problem and prescribed an upper GI, which was scheduled for the day after my Observation.

I was sleeping poorly and drinking too much. In the basement of our home, Mrs. Kessler was filling boxes with her belongings and stacking them to the ceiling. She worked silently into the night after we ate our evening tofu and I washed it down with gin. I could hear her laboring as I stared at the ceiling above my bed, heavy-headed from gin and thinking about my meetings and my upper GI. My only consolation was my imminent retirement.

A remarkable turn of events occurred, though, when I met in the principal's office with Mr. Latovick and his people from downtown.

The teachers union sent Joe Brady, a young man with an ingratiating smile, to represent me. He and I had a conference in the library just before the meeting that would determine if I were a cheat and worthy of censure, or worse. Confidently, Joe munched sunflower seeds, compiling a sizable mound of shells on the library's table, and he chuckled as I explained the circumstances of my case. He had the habit of referring to the School District as "the bastards." "So what did the bastards do then?" he'd ask. I found his casual manner disconcerting because the meeting with Latovick had become for me the most frightening of my three impending meetings, because I imagined it involved my livelihood, my very survival—my pension. The other meetings I could shrug off by reminding myself that I soon would be retired, and then I could tell everyone to kiss my ass. But I had convinced myself that, as a result of Latovick's investigation, the School District could somehow revoke my pension on ethical grounds, and I wouldn't get a cent when I retired. I spent countless hours of insomnia rehearsing in my mind what I should or should not say at this meeting to keep myself out of harm's way, and I debated with myself which lies were most likely to float and which were too flimsy. I even considered throwing myself upon the mercy of the court by prostrating myself on the floor and begging for clemency. Latovick, I reasoned, would love that. But when I told my version of the story to Mr. Brady—especially the part about my fearing the revocation of my pension—he found it all very amusing. He crunched away on his sunflower seeds and laughed with delight throughout our conference and didn't stop laughing until we were on our way to the principal's office, and I couldn't tell whether he was laughing at "the bastards" or at me. He pulled himself together just before we entered the principal's office. "Let me do the talking," he said. "You sit still and say nothing."

When we arrived the meeting was already underway, and the principal was addressing two august persons who stood behind a chair whereon Mr. Latovick sat cowering. These persons—a man and a woman in expensive suits—listened politely as the principal appeared to be accepting their apology for Mr. Latovick's behavior. "I'm sure Mr. Latovick was just trying to get to the bottom of a difficult situation," the principal was saying as Joe and I found our chairs. Then the principal introduced everyone, and I learned that the expensive suits belonged to "counsels for the District." The counselors knew Joe Brady and gave him the friendly nod intimates share in formal settings. After these introductions the principal asked Joe if he had anything to say, and Joe made a speech in which he praised my many years of self-sacrificing service to the District. He remarked how there were no unseemly disciplinary reports in my employee file, and he said that I was approaching retirement after what amounted to an exemplary career of forty years, and that I had taught the most difficult subject of all, English, in some of the most difficult schools in the District, for which "myriads of children in Philadelphia were indebted to me." And the others nodded, including the principal. But my eyes were on the wan Mr. Latovick who seemed to be squirming in his chair, like a small white worm in the throes of death, and he seemed to have been told, like me, to keep quiet, because he said nothing. All he did was sit and squirm.

One of the District's counsels congratulated me on my retirement, and I was about to thank him, but Joe tapped my arm before I could say a word. Then the principal said he would write a disciplinary report about my misbehavior and put it in my files, and everyone agreed that this was a satisfactory conclusion to the business. Latovick looked upward discontentedly, as if to make one last plea to his superiors, but he thought better of it and retreated.

Once outside I asked Joe what had just happened, and he said he had spoken with "the bastards" before this meeting and was expecting this outcome, but he didn't want to tell me this until he was sure. He said that I should expect shortly to receive in my mailbox the copy of a disciplinary report, "a 240," which would reprimand me for my misbehavior, and that would be the extent of my punishment.

"That's it? That's all?" I asked, hardly believing how I'd dodged this bullet.

"Yep," said Joe, "I have saved your pension, and for doing so I expect you to remit ten percent to me." He laughed. "And, by the way, you can have the 240 expunged from your file after two years."

"I won't be around that long."

"Lucky you."

Joe shook my hand and went on his way, returning to his sunflower seeds, and I returned to my cell beneath the stairs, feeling lighter but thoroughly confused.

My meeting with Mrs. Merriwether took place the next day, and it too was anticlimactic. Our school's disciplinarian, Mr. Squires, conducted the meeting in the Boys' Discipline Office, which was a gloomy, undecorated room, more institutional than academic. There was a poster featuring an entertainer I did not recognize admonishing students to abstain from drugs, and another poster of a cartoon character informing students whom to call if they were bullied, but other than that, the room was bare except for a table with chairs and a phone. It had the look of a police interrogation room.

Mr. Squires and I had taught together at Humphrey Junior High back in the eighties. He was a gym teacher from way back when gym teachers worked with a different set of rules than those of us who taught the academic subjects upstairs. The all-male, militaristic environment of the old gymnasium allowed a boys' gym teacher to take certain liberties that other teachers would never consider. One of these liberties was the use of profanity. Though Squires no longer taught gym classes, working instead as a full-time disciplinarian and, in spite of the rules of the School District, which forbade the use of profanity (and unconscious to the possible hypocrisy of a school disciplinarian cursing like a Philadelphia sports fan), Squires spiced his language liberally with swear words, as though it were an essential part of his disciplinary arsenal. Poking his head into my closet hideaway a couple of days before our meeting with Gus and his mother, Squires had asked, "What the fuck did you do now, Kessler?"

"It was an accident," I said. "It slipped."

"You always were a fuckup. Don't you read the fuckin' papers? Don't you see what the fuck's going on?"

"I didn't mean anything. I... I... I..."

"Balls! There's no fuckin' excuse. Unless you were shit-faced or something. But don't get your shorts in a knot. I know Mrs. Merriwether. She's a bitch, but she's a reasonable bitch. Gus is a piece of shit, and she knows it. You just shut the fuck up and let me do the talking. God, you're a fuckup." And he left, mumbling something like, "Fuck me if I want to get involved in this shit."

When I arrived at the meeting, Mr. Squires introduced me to Mrs. Merriwether, who wore the uniform of a bus driver. She sat beside Gus, who occupied himself with a video game on an iPhone. Mrs. Merriwether was impressive in size and demeanor. Except for her formidable bosom, she was built like a man, and her uniform was identical to the uniform of a man, with trousers held up by a thick leather belt, and a chain, like a dog's chain, extending from her belt to her wallet. She also had a man's haircut, but not the haircut of a modern African-American man, more like that of Little Richard in his heyday, a conk. When I sat at the table, she attempted to stop Gus from playing his video game by giving the device a gentle push downward, but Gus moved the device aside and continued playing. Mr. Squires said, "Just let him play; it'll keep him quiet."

Squires began the meeting by expressing how sorry the school was for this incident, and how I had used the "unfortunate term" accidentally (Gus was about to refute this idea, but his mother stopped him). Squires explained how I thought Gus had stolen something, and the word slipped out while I was reprimanding Gus for the crime. He told Mrs. Merriwether that Gus was innocent of the theft (Gus said, "Damn right"), but that I did not know that Gus was innocent at the time. Squires said he'd had a meeting with me during which I'd shown real remorse, both for falsely accusing Gus and for using the objectionable term, and he said I would apologize personally. He turned toward me, indicating that it was my turn to speak, and I was more than ready to apologize, but Mrs. Merriwether cut me short.

"No, no," she said, "this ain't no apology-and-out offense. This is serious business. This man did something that no teacher should do. What kind of teacher uses that kind of language with a student? This man needs to be fired or something. I need to know that the school has punished this man to the full extent of the law," and she pointed at me. Gus nodded abstractly while he thumbed his gaming device. His mother continued. "If someone came on my bus and said that word to me, I'd know what to do." Mrs. Merriwether balled up her fist and shook it a few times. I felt a bead of sweat roll down my forehead. "It ain't right!" she said.

"And for a teacher—No!"

Gus laughed and said, "Oh, shit." Either he approved of his mother's handling of the situation, or he had scored some well-earned points on the device that held him captive.

Mrs. Merriwether glanced crossly at Gus, her temper rising. She was losing patience with him. She pushed his game away from him a bit harder. Gus said, "Naw! Naw!" and continued to poke at the iPhone.

Understanding his position of weakness in my defense, Squires defaulted to what he did best. He cursed. "Well, what the fuck do you want us to do?" he asked. "We can't fire his ass. Just like you, he has a union. He made a fuckin' mistake."

I was surprised that Mrs. Merriwether did not react to Squires's use of profanity, but accepted it as though it were the nuance of an old friend. "First of all," said Mrs. Merriwether, "I want the principal in this meeting. This is too important for just you and me, Thomas. Tell Mr. Hirshburg to get hisself down here. What kind of teacher calls a student a nigger? It's irreproachable."

"Reproachable," I corrected.

When I said this, Mr. Squires looked toward the heavens, seeking help.

"What th—" Mrs. Merriwether stood, knocking over her chair. She turned toward me, her eyes widening, her fists balled. She breathed heavily. Gus stopped shooting aliens for a moment. I felt like I was about to be thrown off the bus. She pointed at me and said, "This man is a menace! A disgrace to his profession! Bring that principal down here—" But before she could reach the apex of her anger, Gus, impressed either with his mother's wrath or his video game, chimed in, "Oh, my *God!* This is the *shit!*" and he laughed hysterically. At which, Mrs. Merriwether, stopped facing me and turned on her son. "Don't you dare take the name of the Lord in vain," she said, "and put that goddamn phone away. How many times have I told you not to be disrespectful to adults! And not to play with that phone when you ought to be paying attention. Here, gimme that phone!" And she lurched toward Gus as if to take his iPhone. Gus pushed back, defending his device and sliding his chair all the way to the wall as his mother grabbed at his phone.

Mr. Squires stood and attempted to calm Mrs. Merriwether, saying, "What the fuck, Violet? You're losing control."

Mrs. Merriwether forgot all about me. She dove at her son's device a few times, but he hugged it tenaciously, and then she stopped grabbing and went slack, letting her anger drain. She adopted the attitude of a disappointed mother, extending her arms toward Gus, saying, "What am I going to do with you, boy? I'm up here at school every other week. You've been in trouble since the third grade." And she turned to Mr. Squires. "He's a smart boy. You know that." Squires nodded, "Or else he wouldn't be here. Never had to do any homework in junior high school and got all A's. But now his grades are so low. So low. And all he wants to do is be funny. What am I going to do?" And while she was speaking, I saw a tear well up in her eye and fall down her cheek. Mr. Squires motioned to me to pick up Mrs. Merriwether's chair, which I did, and he handed her a tissue. Squires led her to her seat and she sat. We were silent for a moment, while the ample bus driver sobbed.

Squires looked my way, "Say you're sorry, Kessler."

"I'm sorry," I said.

Mrs. Merriwether, daubing her eyes, said, "I'm not finished with you."

Squires looked at Gus, "Say you're sorry, fuck-knuckle."

"Oh, my *God!* You made my moms *cry*," said Gus.

Squires caught my eye and nodded toward the door, indicating it would be a good time for me to leave, which I did. I heard Squires say, "No, Gus, *you* made your mother cry. Now hand over the phone," and they continued talking as I left. I don't know what else they said. I assume the conference turned into discussion of Gus's behavior instead of mine, which was a discussion that had probably echoed around that stark room many times. For the rest of the year I expected to hear from Mrs. Merriwether and face the music for my offense, but it never happened.

While we are on the subject of dodging bullets, I should mention that when we issued report cards, not a single parent nor a single student complained about the grades I'd invented from thin air.

14. Visitors, and Dr. Spore meets the Devil

BEFORE Ms. Schlect returned to observe my teaching, I crafted a lesson based on what I had seen by spying on Mr. Wood's class, and I kept the materials for the lesson in my drawer ready for Frau Schlect when she clicked into the room. I hadn't taken the time to carefully prepare a lesson in years, and I could see why. It was so time-consuming. I had to find all the materials and pre-read them and prepare all the handouts and write an outline for what I was going to say.... I almost fell behind in my campaign to finish grading all my students' tests during the school day, and I almost had to take a few stacks of papers home, which would have interrupted my drinking schedule. Only with a struggle did I manage, sitting in my library closet and working feverishly, to contrive the necessary lesson and grade enough papers to allow me to maintain my record of never taking any work home. When I caught up, though, I had an unfamiliar feeling of comfort, knowing that I had a prepared lesson ready to execute, and it was a good feeling.

But when Schlect came to visit, she only stayed five minutes, and she did not write a thing on her clipboard while she sat in the back of the room. She seemed preoccupied and impatient to leave. A few days later, I received an Observation form with no written comments, just a series of check marks in little boxes, and Schlect deemed me "satisfactory." Apparently, my impending retirement changed everything. I had become a dead man walking, not worth the effort of an Observation. I could have read the newspaper while my students chatted at their seats and gotten the same results. But I went ahead and taught the lesson I'd prepared for Schlect's benefit.

After Schlect left the room, aborting the Observation, my students noticed the difference in their lesson. Trying to settle into her place and get comfortable, pregnant Missy asked, "Mr. Kessler, why are you talking so much?"

Brendan responded, "He was trying to impress the vice principal."

Everyone laughed. Me too. Then I continued the lesson.

Harvard-bound Kim, either from extreme guilt or fear of repercussions for her crimes of unlawful entry and theft, visited my cell beneath the stairs in the library at least three times. First, she came with a box full of the items she and Lorraine had filched from my drawers and asked for forgiveness, which I gave. The next time Kim visited, she sat on a stack of magazines and cried like a child while she begged for more forgiveness, saying the whole ordeal was "eating her up inside," and I was so uncomfortable about sitting so close to someone that was crying that I repeated, in every way I could think of, that I forgave her—I almost even touched her shoulder, something I would never consider doing, touching a student—especially a female student. Flustered, I just left the closet and let her cry alone. A few days later, she came for a friendly last visit and we chatted about her plans for the future—the usual stuff, whether she should suffer through the financial burden of medical school, or get a degree in public health or hospital management and make money right away. Doctoring is a good profession, I told her, "Doctors never want to retire." After that, I suppose, she resumed the focus on her goals that had made her a grown-up at age nine, and she left me alone.

With my various tangles untangled, except my rift with Mrs. Worthington, I resumed the invisibility and monotony that had sustained me throughout my career.

The upper GI my doctor prescribed came back negative. When I visited the doctor for my results, for some reason that still bothers me but which he did not explain, he asked me how much liquor I consume on a daily basis. I weighed the consequences of lying against those of telling the truth and responded judiciously, "Two drinks." I refrained from mentioning that each drink contained three ounces of gin or, lately, more, and I was relieved when the doctor accepted my response and simply said, "Ah." He did, however, give me a brochure called "Facts About Alcohol," which I deposited in the waste bin on my way out of his office. After visiting the doctor and hearing him pronounce me disease-free, the cramps in my chest subsided to a tolerable level, and my rampant heart palpitations ceased. I reverted to my old self; namely, suffering only shortness of breath and an occasional irregular heartbeat.

My last days in the system started to fall like dominoes.

Meeting Miss Rigg one morning in front of her class as I was leaving for lunch and she was taking over the room, she stopped me and gave me a mutant banana as a peace offering. It was two bananas stuck together in one peel, like Siamese twin bananas— a real oddity. "When I saw this, I thought of you," she said, and when we fumbled with the banana a little in the exchange, and it almost fell from our hands, her students laughed. I heard Gus say, "Oh, my God, a double banana to do double bid'ness!"

The day before Mrs. Kessler permanently moved herself and her things from our home, she disappeared. Her belongings were packed in boxes stacked in the basement, and she had stuck a Post-it note that said "Mine" on all the pieces of furniture she wanted the movers to take. I didn't know where she went, since our channel of communication had closed, but the next day, while I was at work, her movers came and did a job so tidy that, when I came home, it seemed as though nothing had happened, except there were a few pictures gone from the walls, a few missing pieces of furniture, and a room upstairs with absolutely nothing in it. I rummaged around the house and found some old discarded pictures to cover the shadows of the missing pictures, and I moved some furniture around, and I closed the door to the empty room upstairs, and in one hour I was able to resume my normal routine, martini in hand, though the circus poster I'd hung behind the couch did not compare to Mrs. Kessler's oil painting of rolling hills with a creek running through. There was nothing in the refrigerator to eat, except a bar of tofu and a green pepper, so I sat on the sofa, beneath the huge face of a Ringling Brothers clown, with a cube of raw tofu in one hand and a green pepper in the other, and that was my first bachelor dinner.

That night, I was alone, like a character in *One Hundred Years of Solitude* (a book we read in senior English, and which I liked very much because it took so long to read and required so much plot review). Over the years, through neglect, I had lost touch with every friend I ever had, so there was no one to call who might commiserate with me. They were all Mrs. Kessler's friends. I had merely tagged along to social events. Soon I would leave the teaching profession, and I would not even have acquaintances. I was a loner.

Gosh, I thought, *and I don't even like myself.*

One morning Mr. Wood came to visit me in my cell. Luckily, he'd already eaten his lunch, since the small space of the closet would hardly have accommodated the fragrance of his famous sandwiches. He did consume a package of chocolate Tastykake cupcakes as he sat on a pile of discarded magazines, and when he bit into the chocolaty tidbit, I felt a sharp pain shoot through a salivary gland, and I drooled.

"Nice computer," said Wood, tapping the top of my antique, "a classic."

"No," I said, pointing to the name below the floppy drives, "it's not a Classic; it's an SE."

"But it's a classic even if it's not a Classic," he said.

"Have you ever used a Classic?"

"No, I went from IIe to LC."

"I had an LC 475."

"Good old System 7, right?"

"Yeah, 7—I used 7.2, I think. Remember 8... and 8.5?"

"Yes, 8.5. Wasn't there a problem with System 8 until they released 8.6? Now 9, System 9—AppleShare—that was a system!"

"System 9. Good times," he sighed.

Succumbing to technology nostalgia, we sighed a simultaneous sigh, and Wood asked, "Where's your laptop? This SE must have, what, maybe twenty megabytes of hard drive space."

"It may have forty. I'm only using it for grades." Then I surprised myself. I confided in Wood, "I broke my laptop. Dropped it. Ker-plow. It's dead. I put all the pieces in my bottom drawer. My plan is to give it back and hope for the best just before I leave at the end of the year. I'm retiring, you know."

"Really? Retiring? You lucky dog! I have fifteen years left. What will you do? I think, when I retire, I'm going to get in my car and start driving and not come back for two years. Just lock up the apartment and take off. I'm not married, you know, and I have no responsibilities. I might go to Europe for a year. Taste the wines of Spain and France, live in Paris. What do you have planned?"

"Nothing yet."

"Nothing? Better start planning. Teachers are like medieval serfs. They do not live for the here and now; they live for the here-after; they suffer their gloomy lives on earth, teaching school, so they may enjoy the golden heaven of retirement. The payments we make to the pension fund are the indulgences we pay to buy a place in Heaven... How did your Observation go?"

"Ms. Schlect only stayed five minutes," I said.

"That's great," said Wood. "She only does that if she trusts you. And what happened with Gus and his mom?"

"Squires handled it. It may have blown over."

"Montaigne said his life was full of misfortunes that never happened."

"Except I can't face Mrs. Worthington. And Gus is still Gus."

"Gus is a riot. I saw him the other day running down the hall-way, and there was a girl behind him in hot pursuit, and she was holding her boobs while she ran because they had been set free. Gus had somehow stolen her bra, and he was making a hasty, hi-larious retreat, waving her bra as he ran through the hall. You know, I've been thinking recently about an incident that happened back at Peale at a time when the school was going to the dogs...."

Uh oh, Wood was going to tell a tale and I did not have my tape recorder. I never thought I'd need it in my closet.

"Could you hold that thought for a moment," I said to Wood, who had gotten comfortable, sitting on his pile of magazines and leaning on the wall, "I'm going to make a quick visit to the bath-room, and then I want to hear what you have to say."

Wood nodded as I shot from the closet to my room where Miss Rigg's class was in session. She had rearranged the seats into a large circle, and she was in the middle of the circle acting as a sort of wheel-of-fortune arrow. When she pointed at a random student, he had to continue the progress of the class's discussion, which appeared to be about *Romeo and Juliet* because as I passed behind the circle, a student was saying something about Tybalt changing everything. I thought, *The things they teach in teachers' college these days*, since Miss Rigg was expending enough energy to teach a whole week's worth of classes by running around like a nut in this one class. But I didn't have time to consider Rigg's inefficiency. Now that retirement was imminent and I had earmarked Wood's stories as my retirement-hobby, recording them was all-important. When I exiled myself from the English office, I thought I was doomed never to hear another story, and now Mr. Wood was ready to drop one in my lap. I stole behind Miss Rigg's circle of students unnoticed and found my small tape recorder in my desk drawer. I prepared the tape on my way back to the library, where Wood still sat. He said, "That was fast."

"When you get to be my age, you don't have much to pee. You were about to tell me about Peale going to the dogs...."

"Yes," said Wood, adopting that tone of indifference that heightened the lunacy in his stories. "There came a time when Charles Wilson Peale High School descended into chaos, just fell apart. Things do fall apart, you know," Wood philosophized, "and much more easily than you might think..." He continued:

Peale foundered like a flimsy rowboat in a typhoon. There was one disruption after another, until the place was unrecognizable.

First, we lost the principal who had led the school successfully for a quarter of a century—the Good Old Man. With him went his team—his generals and many of his foot soldiers. They all retired, ran away as though they sensed a gathering of clouds. In the Old Man's place came an energetic young fellow who had a penchant for change but, unfortunately, a penchant for selecting the wrong people to help him make the change. He changed the organization of the school so quickly and dramatically that everyone was disoriented. And he placed the most unlikely people in charge of all the new programs. Many teachers were skeptical about these changes, and they transferred, as though they too could sense something sinister in the air. Then, incredibly, the new principal, the innovator, left, leaving all those unlikely leaders he had selected in charge of the school. There followed a succession of interim principals. Each new principal had a new idea, but each was less effective than the last, until the school had no foundation. Everyone forgot the Old Man's rules, and the new rules were unreliable, ephemeral, and weak. It was every man for himself. The school's reputation was ruined. We could not attract recruits. We fell on hard times. We were like actors without a director, characters without a story, a town without laws.

And this all happened at a time when students were coming to school with worse problems than ever, from increasingly poorer home situations, influenced by increasingly cruder media—children raised far more often by other children or no one at all. The neighborhood was degenerating, and the District began to dump its juvenile delinquents in the school. The place was crawling with bad kids, like never before. Parents of good kids got them out when they felt the impending doom. It was a lethal combination, bad kids and no leadership.

Along came Dr. Spore, recruited from somewhere in the Midwest. She took over as permanent principal, though she never scheduled a meeting to introduce herself; she just sprang up, all of a sudden, like a dandelion.

She was tall and well built, with flowing robes of striking designs, and she wasn't bad looking either—except, when she smiled; her smile changed her whole appearance. Smiling, she bore a striking resemblance to Knucklehead Smiff, the goofy wooden dummy that worked with Paul Winchell and Jerry Mahoney. She had a huge, broad smile, full of randomly ordered teeth. And she crossed her eyes a little when she beamed that smile. It made you want to smile back and then laugh out loud, if you dared. As long as she kept her mouth shut, she looked every bit an imposing professional, but when she smiled, she revealed the wackiness within.

The first time I met her I sensed trouble.

She met me in the hall one day soon after she was installed and, since I had a reputation for knowing something about computers, she stopped to chat. "Oh, Mr. Good," she said, "I need some information. As you know, soon all the computers in the school will be wired up. Can you tell me what inference structure we will need so students may begin surfacing the information supernet?"

"Am I hearing correctly?" I wondered. Notwithstanding Dr. Spore's malapropisms, I answered her seriously. After all, she was serious; she seemed dignified, and I was thrilled that she

had an interest in technology. I gave her a lengthy explanation of the hardware and software I thought would do the job. And she took copious notes. It looked like she wrote every word. Trying to conclude, I said, "I think the solutions I have described will be expensive but well worth it."

"Yes, thank you, Mr. Weed. What department are you in?"

"The English department."

"Excellent," she wrote that down too. "I'll tell you what, Mr. Good, faxcilitate a memo to me with this information, so I can have it violated." And then she flashed that Knucklehead Smiff smile at me, but it may have been too fast to register at that time. She wheeled around and I was left with a mixed impression. A real technophile, I thought, but she might need a good secretary to edit her memos.

For months after our meeting, all I heard was grumbling about Dr. Spore's performance. People said she never came out of her office, that she had lengthy meetings with consultants from outside the school, that a fancy caterer catered these meetings, and that she neglected her regular duties. We were disappointed that she would not address the problem of discipline. Half of the students were arriving late to school. They came and went from classes as they pleased. There were always groups of students in the halls and stairwells during classes. They gambled, cursed, propositioned, and fought in every corner of the building, while Principal Spore seemed more interested in throwing expensive parties in her office and entertaining consultants.

On my way out of the building a few months after our first meeting, I encountered Dr. Spore a second time, and it was then I knew for sure we were in trouble. I met her as she was emerging from her office with a coffee percolator in her hand.

"Ah, Mr. Wang," she said. "I've been looking for you."

"It's Mr. Wood," I said, "I thought you might have forgotten about me. Did you get my memo?" I had spent hours designing a computer system for the school, and I had faxed it to her as she had requested.

"Memo? Memo? Oh, yes, if you sent a memo, I certainly received it. It must be in my 'in' basket. I will rebound directly," she assured me, and with that she flashed a huge smile that for the first time I recognized as the smile of the inimitable Knucklehead Smiff. There were those crazy high cheekbones, that incred-

ibly wide mouth, and all those mismatched teeth. I had an urge to laugh, but I restrained it. "Wait a moment," she said, raising a finger to request that I should not move. And with that, she ducked back into her office and emerged in a moment with a notebook in the hand where the percolator had been.

"Mr. Wart," Dr. Spore addressed me, grinning that daffy grin again, "I have been led to believe that you know something about technology. Explain something please. The crust of the matter is, that soon all the computers in the school will be configurated. Can you tell me what we will need so students may begin servicing the Information Supermarket."

Whoa, I thought, this was too much! I felt a weird combination of comic relief and outright fear. Had she just asked me the same exact question as she had asked the last time I spoke to her, except for the slightly different malapropisms?

"Well," I began, and I gave her the same information I had given her the last time, although not with the same enthusiasm, while she, for her part, took the same copious notes as last time, stopping me periodically with the same questions and, the same as last time, transcribing every word.

She was still writing for a while after I finished talking. At last, she stopped long enough to smile that dopey smile, which this time seemed to mock me. Then she wrote some more notes and turned to go back into her office to retrieve her coffee pot. "You science teachers are so clever," she said. "Could you please send this information to me in a faxcimulate for my records?" She returned with her coffee pot, looking at it quizzically as if trying to determine where the water goes. "You are the wings beneath my sails," she said and headed toward one of those water fountains that have a sign next to them that says, in red letters, CAUTION. THIS WATER IS NOT SUITABLE FOR DRINKING.

You're not going to believe this, but she actually repeated the same question to me a third time a few weeks later. She asked the same question about how to get students on the "Information Supermarket," and I dutifully gave her the same information, though in an abbreviated form (trying not to show my annoyance), which she transcribed verbatim, every word, just like the last two times. Then she showed her appreciation for my making my words brief by giving me the biggest, goofiest, toothiest smile yet, taking my hands in her hands and gazing at me while she smiled, her eyes crossing into their corners, until she looked perfectly insane—I think she wanted to make sure I got a good look at her Knuckleheaded face—and I wanted to laugh so badly I turned bright red, but I bit my lip and bore it. "You should teach the mildly gifted students, you know," she said.

Things grew steadily worse in the school. The scuttlebutt was that Dr. Spore had stopped paying the school's bills. For some reason, she refused to spend any money, except to pay for those expensive outside consultants and the catered buffets they required. For a few days, Dr. Spore and her trusted administrative assistant, Mrs. Holmes, went to a weeklong educational conference in Las Vegas, which must have cost a fortune, and this angered everyone. Dr. Spore became an object of loathing until every member of the staff learned to mimic her goofy smile and used it as an ironic greeting.

It was not teachers, but students who suffered worst under Dr. Spore. The school ceased caring about their behavior. It was not unusual for ten or twelve fights to break out in a single day. A few times a gang of students filed into a room, while everyone watched, and beat up another student. The lunchroom was a gambling den, with students playing cards and dice freely on the tables where their greenbacks lay in the open. The fragrance of marijuana lingered in the bathrooms, and there were rumors that wayward girls serviced groups of boys in secret places within the school. Condoms littered the fire exit stairwell. Boys wore hats and sunglasses; girls wore miniskirts and bare midriffs. It was a mess.

We heard something about a fractious meeting between Dr. Spore and the District Superintendent, who was upset when he visited the school and witnessed the horrible behavior of the students. But still, Dr. Spore refused to leave her office, which was always full of salesmen and laughter, and she made no effort at all to establish order in the school.

Then a male student punched a female teacher in the eye and knocked her out. This made the teachers union angry. They wrote Dr. Spore a nasty letter.

Then a student threw a computer out of a window and it landed on the hood of a secretary's car. The secretaries threatened a job action.

Then there was a gang war in the auditorium, fought be-

cause the girlfriend of one boy was talking to another boy. Two students were hospitalized for stab wounds.

Then a student pulled an old teacher onto the floor by his tie and kicked him in the ribs, breaking one.

The newspapers ran a story called "The School Out of Control." The union bore down. The District applied pressure. Parents pulled their children out of the school. Teachers quit. A siege mentality took hold of the staff. Then the bottom fell out....

Principal Spore often sat for hours discussing grave issues with Reverend Davis, who was a teacher in the History Department but also a preacher. Reverend Davis came to school every day wearing a white cleric's collar. His cleric's shirt was gray instead of black, so he was not a Catholic priest, but his shirt and collar were in the style of a priest. I don't know to what denomination he belonged. All I know is that he was a man of God, and he did not mind bringing God into school. When Dr. Spore began to meet regularly with Reverend Davis, the joke around school was that she must be confessing her incalculable sins.

One morning, I came to school particularly early, because I had picked up Ms. Fortunata after she left her car at the dealership for service. Just as the sun was rising, we pulled into the schoolyard and saw an amazing sight: Dr. Spore and Reverend Davis were standing in the early morning mist holding hands— right in the middle of the parking lot. They had their eyes closed as we drove past, and they didn't stir as we slowly pulled into a parking space. Spore and the reverend kept doing what they were doing, holding hands and standing in the parking area with their heads bowed and eyes closed as though observing a moment of silence. Ms. Fortunata and I looked at each other in disbelief, not knowing what to say. "Do you think they're... an item?" she asked. I shrugged. Their posture was not that of lovers, which would have been preposterous, since she stood a foot taller than he, and he was a man of the cloth, and they were unsuited to be a couple in every way imaginable; but yet, they grasped each other's hands with a definite passion, and we could see the reverend's lips moving quite emotionally as they stood in the morning light. If it were love, it was a strange love indeed.

We stayed in the car and watched silently, because whatever they were up to seemed to be something that would be embarrassing to discover. Soon though, as they held hands tighter and tighter, Reverend Davis's voice rose, and we could hear him say, "The Devil must leave this place! I know he is here. I can smell the sulfurous presence of Satan. I command the Devil to leave this place!"

Fortunata and I exchanged looks of amused surprise. They were praying—casting out demons.

Ms. Fortunata was impatient and said, "I'll put an end to this." She was about to interrupt their prayer service, but I insisted we should stay and listen, because this would make an interesting story to spread around the building. Kay agreed.

As Reverend Davis uttered his prayers, Dr. Spore was enraptured, as evidenced by the ear-to-ear smile that covered her face. "I know he is here—Satan, the source of all evil," exhorted Reverend Davis. Kay and I were laughing into our hands, but the pious duo was oblivious to our presence and lost in prayer. "Satan is the source of blasphemy, faction, and strife! We know that he has taken up residence in this place. We've seen his works. It was he who punched Mrs. Smith in the eye. It was he who pulled Mr. Goins to the floor. He controls the hearts of the children in our school. We know the work of the Devil. We know his tricks. And I say unto him now: Satan, you must leave this place and return it to a state of grace! Satan must leave this place! Satan must leeeeave here! Get thee gone, Satan! In the name of the Lord!"

If Reverend Davis's exorcism could not chase Satan from the building, certainly Dr. Spore's toothy smile and her "Amens" would make the Devil laugh himself to death. She squeezed the reverend's hand like a vise and smiled beatifically up to heaven with her biggest goofball smile. This smile went beyond Knucklehead Smiff, beyond Alfred E. Neuman. This smile was all her own. It was way beyond silly, beyond goofy, beyond daffy, beyond anything. In prayer, Dr. Spore's smile entered the realm of the bizarre, and beyond.

When the prayers reached a transcendent fervency, Ms. Fortunata proposed that we'd seen enough, and we could sneak past the reverend and the principal, and they wouldn't notice a thing. After all, their eyes were shut, and the reverend was preaching strong, "Out, Satan! Out, Satan!" And the principal was enraptured, only interrupting her smile long enough to utter an "amen" here and a "that's right" there. And the two of them *were swaying to some invisible music while they held hands. So they were pretty far gone, and Kay figured we could walk right past them.*

We got out of my car quietly and started for the door of the school, which meant we had to tiptoe pretty close to the supplicants. Then, just as we were passing them, the reverend stopped praying. He opened his eyes suddenly and shot a glance just beyond me. "There he is!" he shouted. And I thought, Oh my God, they think I'm the Devil. The principal opened her eyes too, and we stopped in our tracks. But they weren't looking at me. Their eyes fell on a skinny little student who crawled out from under a car that was parked across the lot. The kid, who seemed more frightened than anything, wriggled out from where he was hiding and took off running. "It's the Devil!" screamed Reverend Davis. "Quick! He's getting away!"

The principal pushed me back toward my car, leaving Ms. Fortunata to fend for herself. "Mr. Weld, follow that child!" Spore ordered. She was not smiling now. "He's the Devil!" she said, dead serious. "We must capture him and make him undo what he's done!" Together, the reverend and the principal nudged me back to my car, which was a new six-cylinder Jetta, and they hopped in with me. "He's getting away," said the reverend. "Look, he's leaving the yard." Ms. Fortunata watched, dumbstruck, as I skidded backward out of my parking space like a jackrabbit and went in pursuit of the Devil.

I don't know why I allowed myself to get caught up in this farce, except that the reverend and Dr. Spore were so sure of themselves and their mission that a refusal seemed out of the question, and Dr. Spore, odd or not, was, after all, the principal. Ms. Fortunata, frozen to her spot in the schoolyard, with a look of total disbelief on her face, watched us as we took off after the "Devil."

I recognized the student who ran. His name, incredibly, was Satinsky. He was an unusual child. His ethnic background was indistinguishable. He looked like he might be Vietnamese or African-American or both, but his name was Russian or Jewish, and he did not have a recognizable dialect or manner. He was a kid teachers discussed, who had a reputation for having family problems. I'd heard that he lived on the streets, between foster homes. Yet he always seemed clean and neat, and he was quite charming. I liked him. I had him for English in the ninth grade. He got a "C," though he could easily have gotten an "A" if his attendance were better.

My passengers pointed to where Satinsky was fleeing the schoolyard. "Quick, follow him!" demanded Reverend Davis. "The new Jerusalem will be painless, tearless, and deathless, because it will be a sinless city of God. Go!" As I stepped on the accelerator I told the reverend that I thought the Devil was just a kid named Satinsky, but Principal Davis cut me short saying, "Like a chameleon, the Devil changes shape. Go!" So I flew onto the street to where Satinsky was sprinting away. He was a natural runner, swift and effortless in his stride, but my car was new and frisky. When Satinsky turned a corner, I turned too, against the light, and I kept abreast of the boy as he tried to distance us. He was fast as a puma. "As soon as we rid ourselves of this menace, I will reconfigurate the school!" said Dr. Spore. "Just don't lose him." I turned into a driveway where Satinsky had ducked, trying to elude us. He was no match for the Volkswagen. I stayed right behind him. When he emerged on a street, I followed close, though I swear he was now running at a speed of forty miles per hour.

The rest of the ride was a blur. First of all, the principal and the reverend started talking in tongues, and I couldn't understand a word they were saying. It may have been Farsi or Yoruba or some combination of languages, but it was nothing I could understand. Then, I couldn't believe a kid could run so fast, or so far. He ran all the way to the Schuylkill River without flagging. And I swear my speedometer hit fifty miles per hour a few times during the chase. It got crazy. I chased the kid through streets and alleys, down railroad tracks, through a park, and clear down to the river, while my lunatic passengers chanted their mumbo-jumbo in my ear and my car bumpity-bumped over all kinds of terrain, shaking us like beans in a jar.

When we got to the river, Satinsky jumped in and swam away. He swam down the river, toward the refineries where the Schuylkill meets the Delaware, until he was out of sight. My passengers jumped out of the car and watched, cheering their success on the banks of the river like they'd just won the Super Bowl. They danced around like spirits, their arms held high, chanting, "Thank you, Jesus! Thank you, Jesus!" And Principal

Spore's smile spread to new widths as she celebrated. "We have vanquished Satan! Jerusalem is ours!"

"But...but... He might have drowned," I said, looking out into the river and seeing nothing. The river was as smooth as glass.

On the way back, I did not pay attention to the maniacal celebrations of my passengers. I hated myself for what I had done. Poor Satinsky, I thought, there'll be hell to pay for this.

But it was a funny thing. Though Satinsky disappeared forever, there were no repercussions from his disappearance. I guess no one cared about him because he really didn't have a home, and people were used to his being missing. He just disappeared without a trace, and no one said a word.

However, while we were out chasing Satan into the river, one of our assistant principals, who was an ex-Marine, had tried to break up a fight between two rival gangs. He was standing between the two gangs, when they drew guns and simultaneously shot the assistant principal in the leg and in the hand.

When we returned from our chase, the press, who had descended on the school in our absence, surrounded Dr. Spore and asked her about the shooting. She responded breathlessly, "Satan is vanquished! He will no longer modify our alumni alma mater." This astonished the press enough to let her pass unquestioned. In the building, police were everywhere. There was general chaos. The District Superintendent was there, and he was livid. "Where have you been?" he asked Dr. Spore. When she told him the story of how she and the good reverend had chased Satan from the school to the river, she was dismissed, fired on the spot, leaving us principal-less once again.

Ms. Fortunata approached me and asked, "What happened?"

I shrugged and said, "I don't know. When they started talking in tongues, I lost track." Which Kay took as par for the course...

There was silence, during which Wood glanced at me to note my reaction, which may have been incredulous, because he said, after a pause, "No lie."

"So," I asked, "Did Knucklehead Smiff come before Little Iodine or after?"

"Before," said Wood. "Ol' Ms. Cole was supposed to clean up the mess left by Dr. Spore."

"Did she?"

"She didn't stay too long. Then Mr. Imbroglio was supposed to clean up the mess she made."

"Did he?"

"Nope. That's why I transferred here. I'd had enough."

"And when was it that the students refused to eat?" I asked.

"Oh, that was long ago, during the reign of the Old Man."

"Ah, and who is this Ms. Fortunata who keeps cropping up?"

Here Mr. Wood hesitated. He straightened his back. He began to speak. He stopped. He whisked a few chocolate crumbs from his pants. He began again. He stopped. He looked at his shoes. At last he said, "Kay was... the only woman I ever loved."

"Were you married to her?"

"No. But I was married, once."

"But not to Kay?"

"That would be impossible. She was married to someone else. We were both married to someone else," said Wood, and the bell rang for fourth period. Wood left silently, glad to be extracted from the conversation about his personal life.

On my way to class I congratulated myself for harvesting another one of Wood's stories. I hoped I could get a half dozen or so more and wondered how to entice Wood back into my closet.

15. The secret lives of teachers

WHEN I was a young man, in college and then starting out as a teacher, I read most of the books I subsequently assigned to students for the rest of my career. After I read them, I never felt the need to reread them when I taught them. Until the time I am about to explain, I hadn't, for thirty years, reread a book that my students were reading. I usually depended on Cliff's Notes if I needed to remember what a book was about. Over the years, I accumulated a whole shelf in my closet full of Cliff's Notes (which, like my colleagues, I forbade students to use). By teaching the same books over and over—the ones I'd read early in my career—and conferring when necessary with my friend Cliff, I got by.

When I taught at Humphrey it didn't matter which books I assigned, those dum-dums didn't read them. I generally assigned abridged versions of the classics, like *Les Miserables*, knowing full well that they would not even look at them. Very few students attended class at Humphrey—they mainly cut—and, because those who did attend were always unprepared, I never had to discuss a text or do anything at all clever with a text. I never even had the opportunity to learn whether working with a text was something I could do. I filled the time my students were in class with note-taking. And I never assigned homework. Homework! Perish the thought. I'd have to check it. And besides, they'd never do it. In class, for the benefit of the few students who attended, I displayed

on an overhead projector copious notes about the book we were
supposedly reading, notes gleaned from Cliff. I asked students to
copy what they saw—and "learn" it, because there would be a test,
a true-or-false test (those were easiest to grade) on Friday. I figured if they couldn't, or wouldn't, read, they deserved to spend
their time doing busy work. Besides, they seemed to like copying
notes. It seemed as though it was pleasant for them to kill forty-five minutes of a winter's afternoon copying, or pretending to
copy, what they saw on a screen. On Friday I would give the test,
everyone would fail, and I would go on to the next lesson. I wiled
away thirty years watching students copy notes from a screen and
testing them on what they had copied.

When I was about to transfer to Northwest, I was worried that
this academic-oriented school might require me to assign books I
was unfamiliar with, and that I might actually have to read some
new books. This prospect made me panic; so before I transferred,
I took what was known as an "observation day" to visit Northwest
and see what English teachers were doing. But I did not observe a
single class on that visit. Instead, when I arrived at the school in
the morning, I asked Mrs. Hegel if I could peek into the English
Department's book room, and after I ascertained that there were
enough books in there with which I was familiar, I went home,
relieved.

I tried the note-taking method when I first came to Northwest,
but it flopped. Students were too sophisticated to sit and copy
mindlessly. They complained. But they were not too sophisticated
to read a book in class, aloud, by turns, which can consume a big
chunk of time, and, thank God, they certainly were not too sophisticated to read a portion of a book to themselves and answer
questions. So I assigned books I had read once upon a time, and I
employed those two strategies—reading by turns and silent reading—and I extended my record of never reading the book I was
teaching, along with my enviable record of never taking an essay home to grade. I admit that the work at Northwest was a bit
harder than at Humphrey; I did have to participate more in my
classes' activities, following their reading and answering questions rather than watching them do busy work, but I successfully
managed to maintain my free time after school to pursue my hob-
bies of drinking and watching television, without spoiling my private hours with reading antique books or grading students' awful

expository prose.

However, with six weeks left in my career, I unexpectedly felt the need to read the book I was about to assign, and I decided to teach it as well as I could. I think watching Mr. Wood had something to do with this. I wanted to try his method of teaching things slowly and carefully, and I wanted to see if I could do what he did. Besides, at this point, I was like a distance runner who sprints at the end of the race because when the end is in sight he can take risks that he could not take during the race. I decided since I was so close to the end of my career that I could take some risks. I could risk the likelihood that I would have to take some work home, since it would only be for a while, and I could risk jeopardizing my health if these lessons required effort, since I would have the rest of my life to take a rest.... I guess I wanted to see if this was something I could do.

The last piece of literature for seniors was *Hamlet*, and I decided to make *Hamlet* my swan song; come what may, I would reread the play—for the first time since college—and at home I would postpone martini time until I was finished preparing for class.

I had always taught *Hamlet* as a classical tragedy about a tragic hero whose flaw was that he thought too much. Pretty standard stuff and easy to teach. But my reading of the play this time revealed something else; namely, that it was a play about snooping. Fascinating stuff. Not only does every character in the play, including Prince Hamlet, engage in eavesdropping, but the tragic conclusion of the play is the direct result of Hamlet's giving up eavesdropping and letting things happen as they will, without his intervention. So I decided to teach *Hamlet* as a play about the tragic consequences of snooping, or not snooping.

I'm sure I lectured too much and had the class read aloud too much—and I could not bring myself to change the seating arrangement into small groups and have students talk to each other (God forbid)—and all-in-all, I did things in my own, outdated way, which I'm sure would be much too traditional for the likes of Wood, but the lessons worked pretty well, and the kids paid attention, for the most part.

Though all these fancy new lessons required me to reread *Hamlet* and, worst of all, they required me to stand in front of the class and talk for longer than my customary seven minutes (an interval I actually timed at the beginning of each class to make sure I didn't exceed because too much talk would hurt me), like the long distance runner, seeing the ribbon a short way off, I decided what the hell, and I actually planned new lessons—every day—and taught them, regardless of how long I had to stand in front of the class and talk.

I even assigned an essay based on an essential question—"How does spying play a part in *The Tragedy of Hamlet*?"—that I told the class would be their final exam. And we paid special attention to all the eavesdropping in the play and discussed whether it was malicious eavesdropping or justified eavesdropping. And we found much of Shakespeare's moral reasoning about spying quite ambiguous, and this gave us lots to talk about.

Actually, I didn't plan to grade the final essay. I would take a quick look at each one and extrapolate a grade. My seniors, ready to graduate, had plenty of other grades on which I could base a final grade (minus the ones I lost) and besides, I planned to inflate the grade of each senior as a kind of parting gift—which would assure me that there would be no dissatisfied customers at the end of the year—so the grades were all bogus anyway. I needed the students to take the essay seriously, though, to give them some focus as their school careers ended and to keep them from getting giddy. Although I would sustain my record of never grading a single essay while I taught at Northwest, I could at least say I assigned one.

My classes on *Hamlet* worked out so well I actually wanted Ms. Schlect to come to my class and take a look at what was going on. I thought of sending her a memo, insisting that she provide me with a legitimate Observation. But it was too close to the end of my career to start that kind of business. I could see the ribbon at the end of the race. All this teaching winded me, but the ribbon was just a short way off.

Encountering Wood in the hall one morning, I asked him if he would like to visit me from time to time in my cell beneath the stairs so we might discuss *Hamlet*, and he was keen on this. I bet he wondered what got into me—actually initiating a literary discussion. But he visited a few times, and he gave me some good ideas about *Hamlet*, including the idea that all the lies and deceit in the play make the world of the play a very confusing world for poor Hamlet, and I thought my idea that the play was about snooping supported his idea of confusion. After all, doesn't snooping increase confusion? I mean, if you have done some snooping and know something that someone else doesn't know you know, doesn't that cause considerable confusion?

I hoped that Wood would grace me with another story, and I kept my tape recorder handy when he visited. I was beginning to see how the fanciful history of his previous assignment at Peale had a kind of continuity. And there were a number of questions I wanted to ask him about his experience. I was especially curious about his relationship with the woman in his stories, Kay. Between discussions about *Hamlet*, I tried to get him to talk about Kay, but he was reluctant. "She's still at Peale," he said, and "She doesn't teach English anymore," but that was about it. He did invite me to join him for drinks after school on a Friday, saying his usual Friday drinking partner was indisposed, and I accepted his invitation. He asked if Mrs. Kessler would mind if I stayed out late on a Friday, and, embarrassed to say there was no longer any need for me to ask, I said I'd go home and ask permission. Then I waited a few days and accepted his invitation.

Although I detested going into Center City Philadelphia, where parking was a problem and prices were a problem and I never felt comfortable, I consented to meet Mr. Wood at a trendy bar off South Street where, he said, I would get the best martini in the city. When the time came, I managed to find a parking space near the bar, where a sign read "two hour parking until six-thirty." I didn't know if this meant that after six-thirty I wasn't allowed to park there at all, or I could park for as long as I liked after six-thirty, but it didn't matter since I intended to have a quick drink and be out of the space before six-thirty. Another sign directed me to pay for parking at the nearest "kiosk." Kiosk? I noticed that all the parking meters were gone, and halfway up the street I saw a woman feeding dollar bills into a mysterious green automaton. The city had changed its parking practices since my last visit.

As a light rain began to fall, I took my place in line behind the woman at the kiosk, and I anxiously examined the kiosk's confusing array of slots and digital displays. When it was my turn to feed the little monster, I read and reread the instructions on its face to establish exactly where to insert money and which buttons to push. An impatient line formed behind and the rain fell steadier as I puzzled over the instructions. I inserted a couple of dollars and some quarters in slots, but I fouled up by not feeding enough money, and the resulting card showed I could park only until five-thirty, which was not enough time. So I looked for a way to add forty-five minutes to the card but, after some perusal of the kiosk and some rain-induced consternation—and the youngster behind me telling me I had to start over—I discovered there was no way to add time to a card so, with the help of the people in line behind me, I started from scratch, this time inserting my credit card, since I had no more change, and after I pushed a button a number of times while the rain fell heavier, I had a card that allowed me to park legally until six twenty-five. I was not about to start over again, nor were my damp fellow parkers about to allow me to, and I figured six twenty-five was close enough to six-thirty and I would have plenty of time for a drink. I put the little ticket in my car where the Parking Authority could see it, and I calculated that I'd spent about eight dollars for an hour and forty-five minutes of parking.

The bar was a fashionable drinking establishment, where the bartenders and waitresses wore a replica of the outfits worn by French waiters—white shirt, long apron, bow tie—and the bar itself was a solid oak antique, nicely restored and liberally decorated by some turn-of-the-century wood carver. Behind the bar were glass liquor shelves and a huge mirror framed in the same oak as the bar—very classy. Beneath the rows of high-end liquor, acting as shelf brackets, there were carvings of women, like small renditions of a ship's figurehead. These sirens were particularly buxom, and the artist had taken the time to provide the oaken ladies with realistic nipples. The pendant light fixtures, the tin ceiling, the hexagonal tiles on the floor, and the easy conversation that filled the space—all foretold a ridiculously expensive martini.

Mr. Wood had saved me a place. He was drinking a pint of dark beer. After our greeting, as soon as I sat, the barman appeared. When he asked what kind of gin I wanted in my martini, I looked at the display of liquors and chose the first gin I saw, Boodles, though I generally drank Gordon's, the only brand for someone who is killing a liter a week. I was careful to tell the barman not to shake the martini, that I'm not James Bond, and not to use shaved ice, and I wanted only the zest of the lime for my twist, no white stuff. I thought if I were shelling out twenty dollars for something that costs a buck fifty at home, it better be perfect.

While I listed my requirements for the martini, I searched for irony in the barman's countenance, but I found none. He sped away, and I placed a twenty-dollar bill on the bar.

"So," said Wood, "are you excited about your retirement?"

"Absolutely," I said, though I was a bit ambivalent at that time. I was even reconsidering my decision, especially during the lonely hours of the evening when planning lessons on *Hamlet* in my empty house was a kind of consolation.

"Is Mrs. Kessler retiring?"

"No, she's got a few years to go."

The barman brought the drink, and I was surprised when he did not take any money. The drink passed inspection. The first sip delivered the cold, dry snap of a good martini, so my anxiety about the price subsided somewhat.

"I don't think Mrs. Kessler will retire any time soon. She started a bit later than I, and I think she likes it."

"You don't like teaching?"

"To tell you the truth," I said, feeling the liberating effects of alcohol's initial diffusion into the bloodstream, "I've always hated it. I can honestly say that I have hated every moment I've been a teacher since the day I began. It's not a job for human beings."

"I don't mind it," said Wood, "pays the bills; lets out early; provides a sense of accomplishment...Why'd you go into teaching if you hate it so much?"

"A paucity of alternatives," I said, "I needed money. In my senior year at Temple University, Mrs. Kessler got pregnant. We had been married for a year. I think we were both twenty when we married."

Wood furrowed his eyebrows. "Twenty!"

I concurred with his disapprobation. "I do not recommend marrying and having children at a young age," I said. "Defers dreams. There was only one good thing about it: I would be a married man with a baby when my student deferment from the Army ran out, so I didn't have to worry about Vietnam—I had a hardship exemption, a 3-A. But we were poor, so poor we lived in her parents' basement. They were nice people, but I didn't especially like bumping into Mrs. Kessler's mother carrying her laundry basket downstairs while I was lounging in my boxers on a Sunday morning."

"I guess sex was a challenge."

"More like an impossibility. They never went out of the house. But, if I remember correctly, Mrs. Kessler was pregnant most of the time we lived there."

"What a situation."

"Look at it this way. I got the whole child-rearing thing out of the way early. Actually, I majored in business in college, and the only job I could get when I graduated was as a car salesman. When I was living in the in-laws' basement, I sold Dodges, Darts and the like. But I was a terrible salesman, the worst on the lot. I retired from selling cars after six months."

"Weren't Darts popular?"

"Extremely. That's how I knew how bad a salesman I was. All the other salesman were selling a few Darts a day, and a Polara now and then. But not me. It was like I was cursed. The lot boy sold more cars than I did."

"I had a '78 Challenger at one time."

"Nice."

"It was like Frank Booth's car in *Blue Velvet*. Black. But it's racing days were over by the time I bought it."

"Well I couldn't sell a Dart, let alone a Challenger or a Charger. So when the Chrysler people dismissed me, I went to work as a substitute teacher. And I liked the short day. It was eighty hours a week on the car lot. So getting out of school at three o'clock was appealing. I went back to college at night and got a teaching degree while I subbed. Actually my teaching certificate is in "Reading" not "English." At the time, I could use more of my business credits for the reading certificate than for English."

"You're a reading teacher?"

"Yup. Back in those days they were dying for reading teachers. Got a job in a snap. Know what my salary was when I started? Six thousand dollars a year. And that was a fortune. I could afford a car, an apartment, and a family on six grand back in '68. And teaching would assure my draft deferment."

This was a good martini. Before I knew it I'd drained the magical liquid and thought it must have been very small to disappear so quickly. On cue, the barman appeared and we ordered another round.

"I've always despised teaching, though." I said, "I cautioned

Mrs. Kessler not to go into it, but she wouldn't listen." Mentioning Mrs. Kessler was a mistake, I realized. I needed to keep the conversation clear of Mrs. Kessler, which would naturally lead to a conversation about my marriage and perhaps even my estranged relationship with my son Hank and, under the influence of gin and in these unfamiliar surroundings, I didn't think I could keep track of all the lies I would have to tell to skirt the issue of Mrs. Kessler's recent disappearance. Besides, my intention was to find out about Wood, not for him to find out about me.

"Oh, come on," said Wood, "teaching is an honorable profession. Think of all the young people you've helped."

"No," I stated with drunken animation, "it's a killer. Teaching has killed me. I mean, it killed me inside. Every day when I go to work I feel like a marionette or a ghost, like I'm sending my body to work while I stay home. I'm glad I'm retiring. I've had it. I feel like I just wasted forty years...for a paycheck. Not even a good paycheck...! Sonuvabitch!"

"Easy there, Arnie," said Wood. I may have gotten loud enough to stop some of the conversation in the bar.

"Sorry. How about you? Why'd you become a teacher?"

"I stumbled into it. Like you, in a way."

At this point the barman asked if we'd be having anything to eat, and before I could say no, Wood had a menu in his hands and so did I. I scanned the frightening delicacies described on the pricey menu— Cuban sandwich, Brie in puff pastry, baby back ribs, sliders—all items I dared not eat. I was hungry, though, and tipsy, and I hardly felt like preparing something on my own when I got home. I ignored the few salads on the menu (concessions to women), and concentrated on the items that fell squarely in the dietary hazard zone. Words on the menu like "sizzling," "stuffed," and "caramelized" made me weak and prompted me to think that I owed myself a dinner out, and that I needed to have something to counteract the booze, regardless of the calories or the price, and the descriptions of the items on the menu began to sound like poetry, until I felt a longing for something creamy, something spicy and salty, something I could feel in my mouth. I heard the sirens sing, and I broke. "Provincial Sampler," I said. Wood's eyebrows went up this time, and he slapped my shoulder. "Good choice," he said.

"Another round?" asked the barman, taking the menus.

"Sure," said Wood.

"I weighed two hundred and twenty pounds once," I said. "Mrs. Kessler's hobby was cooking."

"You found solace for a job you hated in food, huh?"

"And booze," I toasted and drained the dregs.

"I'd like to meet her," said Wood.

"Who?"

"Mrs. Kessler, you dunce."

"Her cooking is restricted to tofu now. It's all tofu, all the time." Oh dear, I was veering toward the subject of my family again.

"So, it's fruit for lunch and tofu for dinner. How much weight have you lost?"

"Sixty pounds."

"Sixty pounds! Damn, man," Wood inspected his baggy friend and chuckled.

I needed to redirect the conversation. Talking about Mrs. Kessler would definitely damage a perfectly good drunk. "So, you were about to tell me how you became a teacher."

"Well, let's see...when I was in college, I was an English major, and I was enjoying myself, reading books and writing criticism, and thinking I was getting away with something because I was actually allowed—no, encouraged—to spend my time reading books and writing criticism. It fascinated me that people actually thought I was hard at work while I was doing what I considered to be a pleasure. What a deal, I thought, to sit in an easy chair and read—for a living. But around the time I was ready to graduate, it dawned on me that there really was no way for an English major to make a living unless he taught in college. So I went to graduate school."

"Where'd you go?"

"I went to Penn for grad school."

"Penn! Who paid for all this?"

"My parents took care of my undergraduate degree at Lehigh but, when I told them I was going to continue with literature in graduate school, they said I was on my own. They wanted me to be a lawyer. My dad was a lawyer. He defended hospitals. My dad was blind from birth, but he was a good lawyer. Incredibly, he often defended the hospital against the disabled person, even though he was disabled. His disability was probably a great advantage to him. Anyhow, he wanted me to carry on the family business of lawyering, but I was stuck on literature, French and English. I'm certified to teach French, you know."

"Dual certificate? Good for you. Senior career teacher?"

"Yes."

This meant Wood was at the very top of the pay scale. I never went past bachelor's degree myself. This conversation was beginning to precipitate the familiar jealousy I often felt in Wood's company. He must have been earning a good eight or ten thousand dollars per year more than I did, and he was definitely better educated.

"I ran up quite a debt at Penn. I had an apartment and tuition and a sizeable marijuana bill, and that was when I thought about teaching in high school. It was becoming increasingly apparent that I would need a PhD to be a professor, and it would take another five years for that; and the field was so saturated I couldn't depend on it. I began to worry that I might not be able to depend on a job in a college, and if I did get a job in a college I'd be so far in debt by the time I got it that it would take a lifetime to pay it off. So I took the courses that were required for secondary school teaching—just in case. I would have started teaching high school as soon as I got my master's degree, because I was at the end of my tether, but I was saved by Marie, my girlfriend, the girl I lived with, the girl I married."

Wood's tale of his privileged upbringing sounded a lot like bragging to me. I was about to say, "Oh, how lucky," when the barman placed the Provincial Sampler before me and proceeded to explain what was on the plate. Cheese was the feature presentation: There was a soft French cheese (so runny it escaped its rind), a pungent Italian, and a crumbly bleu; and these were surrounded by a worthy supporting cast: a generous slice of liver pâté, a few slices of a vegetable terrine, some figs soaked in red wine, candied walnuts, capers as big as grapes, honey, some kind of fruit jam, olives, and pear slices as thin and orderly as cards spread by a dealer. Here and there a slice of grilled bread was tucked in. I was beside myself with fear and anticipation. "Help me out with this," I requested of Wood, and I dug in.

But Wood continued his story, unfazed by the big plate (most likely still digesting a giant-sized sandwich from lunch), "Marie's father was a vice president at Campbell's Soup—in charge of tomatoes, a very important man. And generous. When we married, he set us up so I could study for my PhD. I was lucky," Wood admitted, "I had patrons—first my father, then Marie's. He paid for everything. As a doctoral candidate, I delved into the influence of Émile Zola on the American naturalists."

While Wood jabbered, he may have taken a slice of pear or knifed an edge of pâté, I don't know; I wasn't paying attention. I was busy breaking a twenty-year fast, and I preferred the French cheese to the French naturalists. *Émile Zola?* I thought. *Wasn't he the guy played by Jose Ferrer walking on his knees in the old movie, or was that Monet?*

"We weren't happy," said Wood.

"No wonder," I said, trying to layer pâté with cheese and a caper, "I think I was once required to read a book by Zola, something about drunks, but I took a pass."

"*L'Assomoir*, yes, that's where the watershed incident actually takes place on a watershed. But I mean Marie and me, we were not happy."

Working artistically on the Provincial Sampler, creating clever combinations atop crusts of bread, I was having trouble paying attention to Wood—until he complained about being unhappy in his marriage. That was worth listening to. "What was the problem?" I asked.

"The problem? The problem was that I never stopped fucking other women."

"You never stopped fu—" Wood's abrupt confession stopped me mid-bite with my cheeks full of pâté. I was stunned until I managed to tuck this information into the category of bragging, and then I could continue. "You mean you jeopardized your marriage to an heiress by chasing women?"

"And my career in academia. I never finished my thesis. Mr. Doubletree discontinued his funding the first time Marie left me and went home. That's when I applied with the School District.... I had escaped teaching high school by getting married; then I became a teacher because I was a lousy husband. But I don't know if I ever would have finished that PhD thesis. It wasn't going well. I didn't have the patience to do all the research. I was a reader. And a pontificator. But not a researcher. High school was my niche, I guess."

"Let me get this straight," I said, "You were married to the heiress of a tomato soup fortune, and you were pursuing a career as a professional student, and your father-in-law was footing the bill for this, but you couldn't keep your hands off women. Is this what I'm hearing?"

"More or less. I had a few girlfriends while I was married."

"But no, no, let me get this straight. The vice president of Campbell's Soup was paying your bills, and you couldn't stop... screwing?

"I'm not proud—"

"But wait. I need to understand this. You were married to an heiress and—"

"All right, already!"

"But why?"

"I didn't feel toward Marie the way she felt toward me. I mean I might have at first—"

"How long were you married?"

"Only three years or so. It was rocky. She's remarried now, somewhere in California."

"How many affairs did you have while you were married?"

The bar had filled up while we were drinking and the din had increased. Our plate empty, the conscientious barman appeared as if by magic to ask if we were doing OK, though I had clearly done better than OK. Throughout Wood's speech, I had found new and interesting ways to combine the contents of the Provincial Sampler until the plate looked newly washed. The barman complimented me on my ability to clean the plate. I hoped to hear that Wood wanted to continue drinking, since I felt bottomless, like I could drink through the night, and I was surprisingly hungry, as though the Provincial Sampler had been an appetizer. So when Wood said he was finished, I was disappointed, and I surprised him and myself, and perhaps the barman, by ordering another martini and a cheeseburger (with fries). Wood stayed seated for a while, drinkless, and concluded his story. He was surprisingly candid once he had a few beers in him. "When I was in graduate school I found undergraduate women at Penn irresistible. There were so many of them, and they were at an age when they were ready for experimentation. If I met a young woman who seemed... willing, who was interested in me, I never hesitated to pursue her. I never let marriage get in the way of that. If she had a pretty face and," here Wood used his hands to express the curve of a pear.

"A nice ass," I found myself saying.

"Well...yes. I was easily seduced. Unfortunately, Marie found me out—every time. I was terrible at sneaking. And she was crushed. She left me a few times. I think she really loved me, though her family certainly didn't."

Wood's confession warmed my heart. I loved hearing how he had failed at something. I felt close to him. Almost close enough to make a confession of my own.

"My marriage was like hell on earth," said Wood, softly. "Marie was always depressed. She withstood my infidelities for longer than she should have. Funny, though, soon after I lost Marie, I experienced a drought. I lost my touch with women. Pretty ironic. Perhaps I wasn't trying hard enough. Until I met Kay."

"Kay's the one in your stories about Peale?"

"That's right. I started an affair with her and I think I actually fell in love. As I never had before."

"Are you still with her?"

"It's complicated. But if I were still with her, she'd be in your chair right now, and I'd be telling her how silly you are." Wood shook my hand, and we had a chuckle over that joke (that was not a joke). He dropped some bills on the bar, but I surprised myself and handed them back to him and said I'd look after the check. I must have been pretty far-gone to do that. He let a twenty fall back on the bar and said it would cover the tip, and I thought, *Oh dear, if the tip is twenty dollars, what must the check be?*

"See you Monday," he said and made his way through the throng to the door.

I ate and drank with less enthusiasm after Wood left. My insatiable hunger, it seemed, was contingent to a large extent on his company. Strangely, the idea that Wood's wife abandoned him really appealed to me—he'd certainly made a mess out of that—and it sounded like his latest romantic interest had also dumped him, and this was satisfying too. But his adventures with women, like his commitment to teaching, bothered me—all of those co-eds, and his admission about falling in love with one woman and breaking the heart of another—these adventures had the same effect on me as his prowess in the classroom and his travels abroad and his education and his bilingualism and his sandwiches....

While I downed my burger, a juicy red leviathan surrounded by a heap of fries, I couldn't help thinking about a nature program I'd recently seen on TV. I remembered thinking about Wood while

I was watching the show. In it there was a herd of red deer somewhere in Norway, and one of the bucks was a weak male with no
mate. He snuck into the harem of the alpha male one afternoon
and tried to have his way with one of the alpha's wives. Unfortunately, the king caught him before he could begin his *amours* and
drove him away—scared him off by bawling and using his antlers
and his hooves. The alpha was a big snorting buck, very scary. The
thing I remember was the expression on the weak male's face as
he was repulsed. It was not an expression of fear. It was more an
expression of loss; there was a look of dashed hopes on his long
red deer face. The beating did not injure him. He didn't even fight
back, just ran away. But his spirit was broken. Every once in a
while for the rest of the program, they'd zero in on the sad-looking
buck, who grew more thin and nervous all the time. Now and then
he sidled up to the harem, but he just sauntered and moped, and
the object of his desire was totally indifferent. And here I was, a
single man eating a hamburger alone in a bar on a Friday night,
like the scrawny red deer, without a life, without a wife. And here
was this Wood, this alpha buck, who couldn't stop fucking. I wondered how far evolution had really come.

   "Anything else?" asked the barman after I had wiped clean
another plate.

   "Yes," I said, "coffee. And I'd like to see the dessert menu."

16. The wages of sin and a bit of redemption

WHEN I found my car that Friday night, there was a fifty-five dollar parking ticket waiting for me on the windshield. I'd paid for parking until six twenty-five, not six-thirty, when parking would have become free, and the meter reader was probably there at six-twenty-six with the ticket. So my night out on the town had cost me more than a hundred and fifty dollars, including my exorbitant dinner and the parking fine, not to mention the eight dollars I had squandered to pay for parking in the first place. But I was not in a state of mind to worry about money as I drove home. The caffeine I'd imbibed did not diminish the effects of the alcohol; it added its own dimension. I was downright drunk. I drove home as carefully as possible, talking out loud to myself through the ordeal, fearful that I would incur a DUI as the natural conclusion to my expensive night out. But no matter how loudly I talked to myself, I started nodding off at the wheel as I drove through Fairmount Park, which seemed as vast as a primordial forest. If the grooves dug into the shoulder of one windy road hadn't buzzed me awake, I would have dipped into a wooded gully. Befuddled, I took a wrong turn that led me into one of the darker recesses of the park, which I did not recognize, and I circled around for quite a while, seeing the same snack shop twice. Lost in my own city, until I emerged gratefully on Ford Road and knew my way. When I arrived safely at my empty house, I celebrated by drinking more gin, only I didn't bother with the rituals of martini-making. I just poured the Gordon's into a glass and sipped, until I felt myself falling asleep at the dining room table. Then I staggered up to bed and flopped, still dressed.

Despite all the nodding off I'd done in the car, I could not get to sleep. Staring at the ceiling, I thought about Wood's sordid story of college sex and it generated in me a kind of drunken fantasy. I pictured him sniffing his way through University City on the scent of a pretty coed, a girl dressed in black tights—tights that stressed the shape of her backside. Dressed in his signature tweed jacket and his blue jeans, Wood easily seduced the coed with exciting tales of Émile Zola. They sat on stools in a trendy bar, and she shook her long blonde hair as Wood romanced her in French. He sipped dark foreign beer while she drank wine. What did he care? His wife might be at home contemplating suicide, in their trendy apartment, paid for by corporate America, but he did as he pleased, like a young prince, like a young potentate. In my fantasy, he made progress with the blonde girl. He'd gone to her place; he'd peeled off her black tights, eased off her black panties, pulled her black top over her head, and revealed her pear shape. In my mind, she clambered, nude except for her black bra, onto the bed, where she turned and waited to be ravished by Wood, who did not appear to be thinking about those who made this moment possible for him. Wood was too busy accommodating the sexual experiments of his paramour.

In an effort to minimize the fun Wood was having in my fantasy, I inserted his wife and her family into the scene. I put them right there in the room on a couch as spectators. But it didn't work. Wood kept on having a hell of a time romping around in my mind and engendering in me an infuriating jealousy that I was powerless to stop. I still wonder why I would embark on a sex fantasy that did not include myself.

The bottom line was this: Mrs. Kessler was the only woman I had ever really known. I'd sown no wild oats. And I never really enjoyed Mrs. Kessler because when we were fat, it took the edge off of sex, and by the time we lost weight, we had lost interest in each other. For me there was no experimentation, no master's degree, no sitting in an easy chair with Émile Zola (Mrs. Kessler took the easy chair with her when she left), and no "sense of accomplishment" in teaching. It was an excruciating night. And definitely the worst sex fantasy of all time.

When I finally fell asleep, around four o'clock, I slipped into a twilight half-sleep, and I endured a repetitive dream. I dreamt I was reading and rereading the parking ticket I'd taken off my windshield, searching for the amount of the fine. I read the ticket again and again, but no matter how hard I searched I could not find any numbers on the ticket.

In the morning, I felt surprisingly unaffected by the previous night's debauch and the inadequate sleep that ensued. I even had a nagging desire for a large breakfast, which I did not prepare—just the usual, toast and coffee. But a couple of hours after I awoke, the hangover I thought I'd escaped nabbed me. And what a hangover it was! In addition to the usual nausea and heavy-headed malaise, my heart felt as if it were struggling to complete each beat. My old ticker, flawed as it was on a good day, felt like it was the engine in an old car that was climbing a series of steep hills on a very cold day and wanted to stall at the top of every hill. I tried lying down, but my heart continued to struggle. I tried drinking water to flush the system, and I tried watching television to take my mind off the issue. But nothing worked. I waited until I felt sharp pains in my chest, and I was sure I was having a heart attack. Then I stumbled out to my car and drove myself to the emergency room of Lankenau Hospital.

In the hospital, after I explained my symptoms, a triage nurse took my pulse and blood pressure. She asked me some questions about my pain and whether I was experiencing shortness of breath. And when I told her that I'd had pain but it subsided, and that I always experienced shortness of breath, she pointed to the waiting area and told me to wait until a doctor could see me. I waited there for a long time, watching CNN on TV. There was a story about J.K. Rowling and how surprised she was with the popularity of *Harry Potter*. There was a story about an Israeli incursion into Gaza. Another about famine in South Korea. A Republican senator lambasted Obamacare, saying we Americans already have the best healthcare system in the world, why change it? I was too ill to take anything seriously. Seemingly, all of the other emergencies in the room were direr than mine. The triage nurse was calling people who arrived after me into the exam rooms before me. The broken leg, the stab wound, even the baby with the flu, trumped my heart attack. When the nurse finally called my name and led me to a gurney in a curtained section,

I sat there for quite a while, until a cheerful doctor listened to my complaints. He touched me with his stethoscope here and there, took my blood pressure while I lay on my side and, after we had a short conversation about how much I'd drunk the night before and about the medications I had taken when I awoke, he told me a nurse would arrive shortly to administer an electrocardiogram, and he left. After the EKG, I waited for another endless spell, until the doctor reappeared and told me he could find nothing wrong. He diagnosed my problem as a panic attack induced by a severe hangover, and he told me never to drink more than two drinks. As a bonus, he gave me the same brochure about the evils of alcohol my family doctor had given me, and he told me what he called his favorite bar joke. (A man walks into a bar with an alligator and says, "Do you serve Floridians?" The bartender says, "Of course," so the man says, "Good, give my alligator a Floridian, and I'll have a beer.") He must have been working on his bedside manner. I thanked the doctor and, after I dressed, I tossed the brochure into a hazardous-waste bin, and went home, where I stayed in bed and drank no booze for the rest of the weekend. I would have taken Monday off, except it was so close to the end of the year I figured what the hell. I planned a lesson on *Hamlet*.

I don't mind an occasional trip to the Emergency Room. I find the atmosphere salubrious, with all that medical gear nearby and all those medical professionals in scrubs milling about. It's reassuring to be so close to those who would be most likely to save my life in a crisis. There are lots of interesting things to see in the ER, too—people run in carrying purple kids; the police haul in victims and perps, sometimes in handcuffs; family members of patients wait in a state of suspense; paramedics wheel in ancient people who look dead. It's an interesting place, full of exciting events, and a contemplative place also, a place where one has time to relax and sort things out. I don't know why everyone complains about the ER. Watching CNN, with all its catastrophic stories and dire predictions, combined with all the sick people all around, gives one a sense of proportion. The ER is OK with me.

On Monday, when Wood asked if I'd like to join him for drinks again on Friday, I told him I'd be delighted. "I haven't eaten so well in twenty years," I told him, which was true, and, "I got a twenty-five dollar parking ticket," which was half true, and, "I was so drunk I got lost in the park for hours on the way home," which was an exaggeration, and finally I said, "I woke up the next day in pretty good shape," which was an outright lie. I sandbagged the part about the ER altogether, and we made a date to meet at the same spot on Friday.

In class that week I experienced something that for years I had heard teachers in teachers' meetings talk about but which always sounded to me like a lot of claptrap. How can I say this? I "connected" or had a "learning experience" with a class. We'd gotten to the scene where Polonius uses Ophelia as bait to eavesdrop on Hamlet—where he says, "Get thee to a nunnery." Polonius wants to prove to King Claudius that Hamlet's odd behavior, his madness, springs from unrequited love. Hapless Ophelia agrees to betray her boyfriend, Hamlet, and participate in this piece of spying. But when Hamlet accosts her, he upbraids her harshly for her treachery. He has done his own spying and he *knows* that Polonius and Claudius are hiding behind the arras and watching Ophelia and him. It was all about snooping. Teenagers are especially sensitive to this portion, since Ophelia chooses to obey her father and betray her boyfriend, a situation close to many of their own experiences.

When we read this scene in class, there were two pretty good readers taking the parts of Hamlet and Ophelia. Rajif, a dark laconic youth, was reading the part of Hamlet. When he got to the part where Hamlet's anger has reached its apex and Hamlet says, "Go to, I'll no more on't, it hath made me mad," Rajif paused a moment and read, "It *hath* made me mad," putting the emphasis on "hath," which was unusual. Usually a reader would read "It hath made me *mad*," as though Hamlet is saying to Ophelia that her behavior has made him angry. But our Hamlet paused, and thought for a moment, as though he were forming an idea, and said, "It *hath* made me mad."

I stopped the class. Rajif's interpretation made sense. "Class," I said, "why did Rajif say 'It *hath* made me mad' instead of 'It hath made me *mad*'?" The class stared at me blankly.

I prodded. "Well, what does "mad" mean if Hamlet says, 'It hath made me *mad*.'?"

Missy, listlessly, answered, "Angry. It means he's angry. It made him angry that she's spying on him, and I don't blame him."

"Right," I said, "But what does "mad" mean if Hamlet says, 'It *hath* made me mad.'?"

The stares remained blank, but these were good blank stares, curious blank stares, not the empty blank stares I was used to. These stares were full of thought. I felt nervous, wondering if I could communicate what I intended. I said, "Class, remember in *The Color Purple* when Shug said to Celie, 'You sure *is* ugly, instead of 'You sure is ugly'? What did she mean by emphasizing 'is'?"

"I remember that," said Jerel, who never spoke. "She meant she heard Celie was ugly before—someone told her—and she was agreeing. That was funny. 'You sho' IS ugly'!"

"Yes," I said, "the emphasis changes the meaning. Now what might Hamlet mean when he says, 'It *hath* made me mad'?"

A few hands shot up, but Jerel was not to be denied. She blurted, "'It *hath* made me mad,' means that something *has* made him 'mad.'"

"Rajif, what does 'mad' mean if Hamlet is agreeing or recognizing that something has made him mad."

Rajif said, "It means he is realizing that Polonius is right. Love has made him mad. He *is* crazy because of Ophelia. 'Mad' means crazy, not angry. It *has* made me mad."

I could see that Missy understood. "Good," I said, "Missy, what is Rajif saying?"

"That Hamlet is surprised to find that Polonius was right, that love is the cause of his madness, and that he *is* a little bit crazy. How ironic."

"But he is angry," said Brendan.

"Yes," I said, "but in Rajif's interpretation his anger abates for a moment. He goes deeper into himself. He realizes that foolish old Polonius has a point... Excellent," I said and I pointed at Rajif and did an exaggerated rendition of his interpretation, "*It-HATH- made me mad.*"

"Jiiiiiif!" someone said to congratulate him on this insight. The class approved. Rajif coolly slipped on his sunglasses.

"Can love make a person crazy?" I asked.

All together the class agreed with a resounding "Yes!" that love could. And right on cue the bell rang—just like in the movies.

When I thought the class had left, I said to myself, out loud, "What just happened?"

Lisa Wong, who was always the last to leave, was still in the room. She sang, "You're so silly, Mr. K. Or should I say, 'You're *so* silly'?" And giggling, she hurried toward the door, hoisting her enormous backpack onto her tiny frame.

The District found the time in the waning days of the school year to administer one more benchmark test, and Mrs. Worthington came personally to my room to give me an Administrator's Handbook. It was early in the morning, before advisory, while only a few unsteady youths were shuffling about the room or sitting in a torpid state eating the pale bagels supplied by the District. Worthington said good morning—she didn't seem angry; in fact, she seemed cheerful—and she opened the test-administrator's guide to some pages in the back. She'd highlighted the bullets that pertained to what the administrator is allowed to say during the test. "Look here, Mr. Kessler," she said, "let's not have any trouble this time. I'm going to review this section with you personally, so no one can say that I was remiss in informing the staff. Now read the portions I highlighted." I read them quickly, saying the important words aloud. "OK," she said, "now answer this question: What are you allowed to say during the test?"

"Nothing," I said.

"Nothing except what?"

"The instructions."

"And if someone asks you a question?"

"Only answer if it is a question about the instructions," I said.

"Good. Can you follow these instructions?"

"Yes."

"Then have a long, healthy retirement," she said, and she smiled broadly. For a moment, she cocked her head slightly and searched my face. Her smile was one I recognized. People often smiled at me like that, though I never knew what to say. Worthington waited a moment, then turned and clicked away. Hours later, in the middle of the day, I realized I'd been given a chance to apologize and muffed it.

17. Wood's last tale

THAT Friday I parked around the corner from the bar and I used a credit card at the kiosk to buy as much time as it allowed, enough time to last well past six-thirty. I was seated at the bar before Mr. Wood arrived. The barman was glad to see me. "Martini?" he asked, and started preparing the drink before I okayed it. It was early, the empty bar was echoey, and the buxom sirens that shouldered the glass shelves were mute. I nursed my martini until Wood arrived and ordered a Guinness.

"How's the *Hamlet* going?" he asked.

"I may have had a teaching experience," I said.

"No," said Wood with a "you're kidding" intonation.

"Here's to *Hamlet*. My next to last book."

"What will be your last?"

"The sophomores read a few of Shakespeare's sonnets and I'm out."

"All things must pass. Figure out what you will do in retirement?"

"I'm thinking about writing a book."

"Really? What kind of book?"

"I don't know yet. Fiction, I think; maybe a novel about teaching."

"I have noticed," said Wood, relaxing, "that people who have returned from some kind of ordeal write the best novels. Look at

Herman Melville who tramped around the South Seas before he started writing, or Günter Grass who lived through—and with— the Nazis, or that crazy Bukowski who was a drunk for so many years before writing about drunks. I wonder if we teachers live through an ordeal worthy of a novel."

"I'm not sure," I said, "though I have heard retirees say they are suffering from a kind of post-traumatic stress syndrome. Maybe I'll write a detective novel. I could invent a quirky detective who is a teacher by day and a private eye by night. How's this: There's this school and the principal has decided to improve the faculty by killing the teachers she finds inadequate. So this teacher has a hunch about what's up and investigates... What do you think?"

"I like it," said Wood. "The principal can commit the crimes in the boiler room. School boiler rooms are gothic, especially the old ones with old coal furnaces."

"You should write a book."

"Me?"

"Yes. You should write a book about Peale High. And tell those tall tales you tell."

"What tall tales? They're all true as true can be."

"Right."

"You don't believe me?"

"A principal who wears a costume to make her look bigger? Everyone suddenly speaking another language? The Devil? Come on."

"What?"

"Gimme a break. The stories are very amusing but hardly believable. A fasting fad? Well, actually that one sounds plausible."

"Tell you what," said Wood, "I'm going to meet my friend Kay at Peale when I'm finished here. She's consented to meet me for dinner which, believe me, took a bit of pleading. We're going to a funky Italian spot in Southwest Philly that still has checkered tablecloths. If you like you can follow me down to Peale and say hello to her. You'll see *she's* real."

"I never doubted she was real."

"Look, I'll do you one better. I'll tell you one of the most incredible stories of them all, and when we go to meet Kay, you can look at Charles Wilson Peale High School—the building itself, and you'll see that I'm not talking out of the side of my neck."

"What do you mean?"

"I'm going to tell you the story of how the building got to be the unbelievable structure that it is now, and when you see it, you will not be able to doubt the veracity of the story."

Once again, Wood was winding up to tell a tale and I did not have my recorder. This time there was no way to retrieve it. I would have to store all the details of the story in my head if I wanted to use it, and this one sounded like it might be a beaut.

Wood interrupted my thoughts. "Let's order another round of drinks, and I will tell you the story of Mr. Imbroglio and the Rubik's Cube. Then you and I will take a trip to Southwest Philadelphia, and I will provide you with evidence that the story is accurate."

"You should really write these stories down—" I said, though I thought, *I wonder if I have enough of these stories to keep me busy for a while?*

"The drinks are on me," said Wood. "Are you hungry?" And no sooner had Wood asked this than the helpful barman plunked down a couple of menus which, though I was loath to do so, I pushed aside. Drinks served, Wood began (I have reproduced this story as faithfully as possible, using the previous stories as models):

Mr. Imbroglio, the principal who came after Mrs. Cole, was married to the philosophy that a beautiful school building was the key to a school's success. His mission in life was to overhaul buildings. The nicer the building, he thought, the smarter the kid. He spent his nights writing elaborate proposals to have Peale refurbished. And he spent his days making phone calls to expedite his proposals. He left his other duties unattended so he could concentrate on the business of renovating the school.

He was successful, too. He attracted enough money to reconstruct the school building entirely, from the ground up.

Without further ado, he contacted the company that would make the renovations, and he ordered them to begin immediately. He calculated he could get the place fixed up without anyone even noticing it, if he did it quickly and didn't tell anyone. He wouldn't even tell his assistant principals. He would just go ahead full-steam. The staff and students, he thought, would live through the hardships of the renovation, which would only last a few months. And then their lives would be so vastly improved because of the beautiful building, they would hardly remember the hardships.

The principal bought himself a special hardhat with the word PRINCIPAL emblazoned above the brim, and he went out into the schoolyard one afternoon to greet the head engineer.

"Let's do it," said the principal with authority as he looked squarely into the eyes of the engineer and shook the engineer's hand briskly.

"Do it? Do it when?" asked the engineer, surveying the building.

"Immediately. Today. Now!" said the principal, increasing the vigor of his handshake.

"But, sir," cautioned the engineer, "you need time to get your people situated—"

"Tut, tut," said the principal, shaking the engineer's hand even more vigorously. "Proceed as though we're not even here."

"But, Mr. Imbroglio," the engineer said, "we're going to excavate the entire building. All the furniture and fixtures will be removed. Walls will be torn down. The place will be rewired and rebuilt. There will be no plumbing for a long time. Your people cannot stay here while the building is in such a condition. It's not safe."

"Nonsense. We had a meeting last week," the principal lied, "and we decided that the school's renovation should not interrupt the educational program. You just go about your business and leave the functioning of the school to us. We'll stay out of your way."

"We're going to gut the place!" said the frightened engineer.

"Tut, tut," said the principal. "Tut, tut."

The next day the renovation began. The engineer wasn't kidding. The construction company gutted the place like a fish. Classrooms full of surprised students and teachers fled into the hallways as men wearing hardhats and masks rounded up all the desks and chairs and hauled them down to the basement. Masked workers pulled down every bulletin board and chalkboard. They treated bookcases full of books like rubbish. The amazed teachers and students watched as books, cassette players, bookends, TV sets, posters, papers, and office supplies accumulated on the floor. The tireless hardhats collected the jetsam of the school and gathered it into huge piles in the hallways until nothing but the bare walls remained in the classrooms.

The students were delighted with the surprise renovation,

and they immediately evacuated the building and went home. Teachers stayed as long as they could and watched, but they soon had to leave too. By the end of the first week, the school was stripped bare, and everyone was gone. A fine chalky dust filled the empty rooms and hallways. The building was uninhabitable.

To the satisfaction of the principal, no one complained.

By the second week, only a few students showed up, and they drifted home when they realized they could not enter the building. One morning when teachers arrived, the principal greeted them in the parking lot and told them to remain outside and gather for a public address. He shook hands with various staff members and smiled. He was delighted with the speedy progress of the renovation. He wore his monogrammed hardhat and a long shop apron, and he carried a bullhorn. At the appropriate moment, he addressed the staff, which had assembled in the schoolyard. From the steps of the school's entrance, he spoke through his bullhorn, while the noises of construction awakened behind him.

"As I speak, history is being made," he said. "Our school is being rebuilt to accommodate the most modern educational paradigms. Fear not. Our programs will not be disrupted by this process. Ultimately, they will be improved. You are being asked to take advantage of this wonderful opportunity by becoming a part of it. During the renovations, school will be held around the corner at the church. During this trying time, it is expected that you will formulate a plan to take advantage of the new school building when it reopens in six months. Remember: A student is only as good as his school building. There will be a few handouts for you to look at so you can formulate wise plans...."

The principal disappeared into the school while some staff members handed out a newsletter called "The Building of Minds" which was a quarterly publication devoted to showing the advantages of renovating school buildings.

Then the teaching staff, along with seven or eight students, trudged off to the small church around the corner to commence with the business of education.

Six months passed. Like most building projects, this one fell behind schedule. There was a problem with the building's design. It was very complex. The plan was for the building to look like a huge Rubik's Cube. The big cube would hold smaller brightly colored cubes, just like a toy Rubik's Cube. What's more, through the use of powerful electric motors, the principal would actually be able to twist and shift the small cubes just as a child might shift and twist his little Rubik's Cube puzzle. The colored cubes that composed the building could be rearranged to allow changes in the structure of the school. For example, at a moment's notice, just by activating the electronic motors, the principal could shift the position of the library so it would be closer to the computer lab. From outside, this shift would look like the school was a big Rubik's Cube manipulated by an invisible hand. Unfortunately, these movable cubicles posed endless problems for the construction crew. And the renovation crawled.

The delay annoyed the principal who was dying to get his hands on the controls of the big cube.

At the church around the corner, an unspoken agreement between teachers and students gradually formed. The agreement stipulated that as long as the school was in a transitional phase, no one expected all that much from their students. The old church seemed so impermanent and so unfamiliar that it was hard to take anything seriously. Everyone relaxed. Besides, the energy of the teaching staff was directed toward what they would do when the renovation to the old building was complete, and teachers spent precious little energy on lessons for the present batch of students. These students responded by showing precious little interest. A careless indifference pervaded the temporary school.

Unfortunately, the careless atmosphere of the temporary school frustrated some of the school's finest teachers, and they transferred to other schools. And the parents of many of the finest students were frustrated too, and they pulled their children out of the school. Some of the school's administration became unhappy with the situation, and they retired. As the construction dragged on, the personality of the school changed, seemingly forever.

At last the construction ended. It was three years overdue. The school was beautiful. It looked like a big Rubik's Cube, and all the modules moved and shifted as they were supposed to. The design worked! The School District donated a nice little garden to surround the new building. On the day of the grand opening, the principal threw a big party complete with a barbecue and a local string band. At the principal's request, the construction company threw a huge tarp over the whole building as though it were a statue ready to be dedicated. Everyone—all of the students and *teachers with their families and friends, along with dignitaries from the School Board and the organizations that donated the money in the form of grants, together with local politicians and community leaders—everyone who was associated with the school—attended the party that marked the school's reopening. It was a fine affair.*

At an appropriate moment, the principal mounted the steps and delivered a simple speech. "Everyone deserves to be thanked," he said through his bullhorn with a quavering voice. "A hard time has been endured by all of us. But in my heart I know the right thing has been done, and our sacrifices will pay off.... It is thought by some that too high a price has been paid for our beautiful new building. To these I can only say one thing: A student is only as good as his school building."

And with his final words as a flourish, the principal pulled the cord that made the tarp fall from the finished building, and the crowd applauded the giant Rubik's Cube. Tears fell from the eyes of Mr. Imbroglio, tears so big they looked like raindrops as they fell on the pavement.

Virtually overnight, the students and staff moved back into the school.

For a time, confusion reigned. The move was arduous; the reorganization was difficult; and the changes were puzzling. The hardest part of all was getting used to the shifting of the cubes. The principal liked to stay late into the night moving the modules around, trying to get all the rooms in the building just where he wanted them. Sometimes, on our way out of the building in the afternoon, we could look into the principal's office and glimpse Mr. Imbroglio in the cockpit he used to rearrange the cubes. He sat in his pilot's chair for hours with his hands on the large levers that effected the changes. He seemed possessed with the various dials on the instrument panel, and occasionally talked to himself and laughed. Unfortunately, when the principal made changes in the positions of the rooms, he gave little notice to the staff, and this created problems. Often the staff would arrive in the morning and find things quite unlike they had ever seen them before. Then a mad scramble would ensue with teachers and students trying to find their correct places. Public address announcements only seemed to make matters worse. And the directions in the daily bulletin were sketchy at best. These were some of the hardest times at Peale High.

After a few years, though, things settled down. Many of the students who had drifted away from the school drifted back. The lackadaisical attitude of staff and students from the transitional phase ebbed away. People lived with the Rubik's Cube and even joked about its shortcomings. Education resumed.

However, something annoyed the principal beyond his tolerance. Statistics showed that the students were not getting any smarter. And Observations showed that the teachers were not teaching any better. All in all, things returned to exactly as they had been before Imbroglio beautified the building. Only now, if anything went wrong, people immediately blamed the renovation as the culprit. The disruption caused by the school's renovation lodged like a painful memory in the psyche of the school, and staff members traced the root of every problem back to the renovation and the time that it took. This burned the principal up.

So he transferred, leaving the big cube in the hands of another man.

"But you didn't stay after that, right?" I asked, empty martini glass in hand.

"No. Like many others, I transferred. But that building is still there. You and I are going to take a ride out there right now, and I will show you the building. We'll be just in time to see Kay, if the traffic's OK." As he said this, Wood waived for the check. "You'll see," he said.

I followed Wood down I-95, past the stadiums, the Navy Yard, and the refineries, until we reached Southwest Philadelphia, where we traversed the industrial fringe of the neighborhood, and navigated into the streets of brick row houses. I lived in a similar row house, but these showed more signs of neglect than those in my neighborhood. There seemed to be a burned-out house on every block. Too many screen doors swung open in the breeze. The lawn mowing was inconsistent. We turned a corner and, like magic, there it was, just as Wood had described it—a huge multi-colored Rubik's Cube rising from a small shrub garden. The cement schoolyard that surrounded the garden was so littered with glass it looked like bottle tossing was the favorite local sport. A warm evening wind whistled through the leafless shrubs at the base of the building, leaving a few empty snack bags in the branches. Shotgun fungus stained the corners of the white Rubik's squares, and some of the squares were chipped. A seagull shrieked in the green twilight. The odd school did indeed look like the faded remnants of some wild-eyed principal's dream. A plaque above the windowless metal doors read Charles Wilson Peale High School, and next to the plaque on a green Rubik's square someone had scrawled the words *"6-o is pussyes"* in spray paint.

"What'd I tell you? There it is, a building in the shape of a puzzle," said Wood.

"*'Pussyes'?*" I asked.

"Creative spelling. Someone is not fond of the boys from 60th Street."

"Do those cubes still rotate, or move around, or whatever they do?"

"Maybe. I don't think anyone bothers with them anymore."

We waited for Kay by the fence that surrounded the schoolyard. Only a few cars were parked in the yard and there was no one in sight. Because the empty space was normally crowded with teenagers and teachers' cars, it had a particularly doleful look in the waning light. I was astonished by the heretofore-unknown huge cube, like finding a hundred-foot waterfall in the park around the corner from where you live.

"Why does Kay stay so late?" I asked.

"She always leaves late. She has a number of extracurricular jobs—yearbook, union rep, department chair...makes a fortune."

"So you would normally have your Friday afternoon libations with her?"

"Until she said she no longer wanted to see me."

"She dumped you?"

"Yes," he said, "in a way." And with this the heavy gray door at the base of the building slowly opened. Wood straightened and waved as Kay emerged. From far away I could see she was a beauty, but close up she was stunning. She had a classical look: wide-set eyes, high cheekbones, plenty of wavy dark hair, and just the slightest unevenness in her front teeth. When Wood introduced us, I could hardly look her in her eyes, she was that good looking, and when she smiled a hello, the imperfection in her smile served as proof that the rest of her was perfect.

Wood and Kay kissed, but in a desultory way, with Wood initiating.

"What a place this is," Kay said. "It gets crazier every day. I think half of my department called in sick, which is not unusual on a Friday. I almost had to cover a class."

"Do the kids come on Friday?" Wood asked.

"Who knows? There are more kids in the hallways than in the classrooms."

"Why don't you transfer to Northwest?" I asked.

"Are you kidding?" Kay was amused. "Too much work." Which was the perfect answer—a woman after my own heart.

"Kay Fortunata, Arnold Kessler," said Wood, by way of introduction.

To which I responded, *"Enchanté"* (which has bothered me ever since).

"Let's get out of here," said Wood. "This place is like the Wild West after dark." And we parted.

Driving home, in an effort to commit the story of Mr. Imbroglio and his building full of cubes to memory, I retold it to myself, but the bewitching face of Kay sabotaged my thoughts. I thought of her crying in one of Wood's previous stories, and I felt like it was not right for someone so good-looking to cry. I thought about Kay and Wood at dinner—with their checkered tablecloth and, no doubt, a fiasco with a candle. A *fiasco*, for God's sake... I hoped they were getting on badly.

18. Kay

IN AN effort to stimulate the U.S. economy, George W. Bush sent
me a $600 tax rebate, and I bought a computer. Damn nice of
President Bush, whose reputation among teachers was uneven at
best, but whose reputation among those who hate taxes was un-
paralleled. The pedagogical ill will toward Bush was due to his
administration's support for the policy of No Child Left Behind,
wherein the federal government forced school districts across the
country to accept testing as the holy grail of everything educational, and a school's entire reputation was judged by its students'
average test scores. As far as I was concerned, the ascendance of
testing as a priority over, say, class management or innovative
curriculum, was a good thing, since my students at Northwest
were handpicked, and they did very well in tests regardless of who
their teacher was, which made me look good. And besides, I enjoyed giving tests, since they gave me a break during the classes
when they were administered—all I had to do was watch students
answer questions—and I could catch up on any paperwork that
was due. I say, God bless George W.

At any rate, I used Bush's stimulus gift to buy myself a new
Apple MacBook, at which I am sitting right now in my writer's
niche. I had been using the school's computer as my own, but
when that one went south, I was operating without a computer
at home. My only computer was the antique Mac sitting on the

student desk in the closet under the stairs in the library, and that machine was essentially a one-trick pony—it calculated grades, and that was all it could manage.

After I purchased this new computer, the first thing I did was spy on Mrs. Kessler by reading her email. This was simple, since I knew most of her passwords, and I knew she used either her School District email account or a Gmail account. Reading her email, which was mainly as tedious an activity as cleaning a desk drawer, I learned that she did not have a boyfriend (how could such a dowdy old soul?), at least not a boyfriend with whom she communicated using one of these accounts, and I found that she was way too involved with the internal politics at her school. On more than one occasion, I wanted to blow my cover and answer one of the messages she sent to her colleagues in which she nattered about her principal, and I wanted to convince her to ignore all the things she couldn't control, like budgets and staffing. There are laws against such invasions of privacy, of course, so I remained covert. I further learned that the thing she most despised in her break-up with me was the complete lack of emotion I showed during the process. She claimed, as though I were one of her students, that I was suffering from Asperger's syndrome, a claim I found insulting, since she did not have the credentials to make such a diagnosis. I looked up the disorder on the Internet and, from what I read, while I could see why Mrs. K might accuse me of having this disorder, those real Asperger's bozos were a lot crazier than I. A real Asperger has no idea how to behave in public. I also learned that she was undecided about how to proceed with the legal end of our separation. I searched for any correspondence she might have with a lawyer, but I found none. I decided that if I just sat tight, after I retired, if we were still legally married, I would become a dependent of hers as far as the School District was concerned, and I could take advantage, automatically, of her health insurance benefits, and this was good. The most annoying thing I learned from Mrs. K's email was that she kept a regular correspondence with Hank, our son in Boston. Though their conversations were superficial, they nevertheless communicated, even though I hadn't spoken to Hank in close to twenty years. I was deeply offended by this, thinking that Mrs. Kessler had appropriated my son through devious means, behind my back. I decided they'd been in regular communication for years, and that she and Hank conspired to form a secret alliance against me, and this was disingenuous and unnatural. After all, I was his father. Did she think I would be a bad influence on my own son? That I would spoil his capacity for emotion or make him an Asperger? Or did she just want to keep him for herself? Certainly, Hank didn't desire to marginalize his father. Although I resolved not to do or say anything that might disturb Mrs. Kessler and jeopardize the valuable health insurance she might provide, I would certainly, at some point, try to contact Hank and find out how his mother had expropriated him from his father. From reading their correspondence, I learned that Hank was working in a test kitchen for a large baking think-tank that supplied information to various suppliers, including the Krispy Kreme company, and that he had been instrumental in selecting the flavor of the jelly in their latest jelly doughnut. He also did some catering work on the side. He and Mrs. Kessler talked about their weight problems, so I inferred that poor Hank had succumbed to the family trait of obesity, and I surmised that he, like his father, had chosen the wrong occupation. A baker with a weight problem might be even worse than a teacher who refuses to make lesson plans. They spoke very little about his personal life, except he did refer on occasion to his roommate Stanley, who sold tickets in an underground booth for the MBTA and, much to Hank's chagrin, suffered from chronic depression. Yes, someday soon, I would send a message to Hank—very soon.

It was so close to the end of the school year that my seniors were losing interest in school. Most of them were accepted into college and, though they were giving lip service to *Hamlet*, their hearts were not in it. I couldn't blame them. I was riding out the last few weeks of school by showing Kenneth Branagh's version of the play, which was over three hours long and, I hoped, would keep them quiet until graduation. I needled them about the final essay, even though I was going to dump it in the trash.

My sophomores, meanwhile, still had a whole month to go, so I went at them with a few of Shakespeare's sonnets. I always liked teaching these sonnets, since they required no preparation on my part, while students needed hours to figure them out. I could review one of these babies minutes before the beginning of class, and then set the class loose for an entire period trying to decode it. The only problem was, I only knew how to decode four or five of them, from reading and rereading them over the years. After I shot my load I would have to spend hours decoding new ones myself. So I generally stuck with the ones I knew, and based a whole literary unit around them. I'd use a recording of Richard Burton reading a sonnet, which I would play twice, and then I'd distribute questions for students to answer. *Voilà!* Instant two weeks of lesson plans.

But now, in my final few weeks of teaching, with my newfound interest in my profession, I was courageously taking the place of Richard Burton and reading the sonnets myself. I was answering questions as I read, explaining difficult metaphors, and discussing themes—things I would have avoided in the past. I actually planned to introduce a few sonnets with which I was unfamiliar, which I was actually preparing at home during martini time. Martinis and Shakespeare went surprisingly well together, I found. I was especially interested in Sonnet 129, "The expense of spirit in a waste of shame is lust in action..." I figured if adolescents didn't understand how their lustful antics were shameful, who would?

Mr. Wood visited me one morning in my cell while I was reading Sonnet 147, which concerned some poor sap who was so smitten by love that he was going nuts pursuing a lady. I was just thinking how the beauteous Kay Fortunata would be a lady worth pursuing, when Wood knocked on my closet door and entered. Crumbs from some crusty loaf dotted the front of his jacket.

"What's up?" Wood took a seat on a stack of discards.

"Shakespeare—kick in the rear," I said, holding up my book. "Sonnets. Sonnet number 147. The poor sonneteer is going crazy with lust." I read: "*Past cure I am, now Reason is past care, and frantic-mad with evermore unrest; my thoughts and my discourse as madmen's are...* Ha ha, what a lulu."

"I'm unfamiliar with that one," said Wood, "but it follows a kind of pattern. Shakespeare is suspicious of carnal love and celebrates the romantic variety, the kind that lasts."

"Not always," I said, "there's one I read about Cupid's arrows, where the narrator seems to be cured by carnal love." And I was proud of myself for parrying with Wood on a literary matter.

"Yeah, well, those sonnets go every which way, I guess. But I came to tell you that Kay will join us for drinks on Friday."

"Oh, good," I said, trying to be as casual as I could. Since I had glimpsed Kay outside her unusual school building, she had taken control of my imagination, and she and I were having quite a good time together in my mind. Though she was twenty years my junior, and I hardly would stand a chance with such a beauty, I longed to see her again. She was infectious. It was killing me to know what the story was between her and Wood and how close they were.

"I don't think she wanted to go out with me until I said I was bringing you," said Wood. "That cinched it. She can't resist a new person."

"She wants to know me?" I asked. My heart sped up a bit. "I'm so happy. People never want to know me."

"Well, Kay wants to know everyone."

"So what's the story between you two?" I asked, my curiosity spilling out.

Wood did not seem as inclined to discuss his personal life in the environs of a well-lit library closet as he was while sitting in a dimly lit bar on a Friday afternoon with his spirits buoyed by two pints of beer. "We're on friendly terms," he said.

"But you're no longer together or whatever," I prodded.

"I guess not."

"But you'd rather you were."

"I guess so."

"So what happened?"

"She changed."

"Changed?

"Let's not talk about it." Wood dusted his jacket and made a motion as if to leave.

It occurred to me that the reason for Wood's reticence on the issue of his girlfriend had to do with the way that I was always asking him for information but I offered none in return. So I spilled the beans. "There's something I'd like to share with you, Roger," I said. "I haven't said anything because the injury is still fresh, but it's like this: Mrs. Kessler left me. Packed her things and left. We had a strained relationship for years, and she decided she couldn't live with me anymore. She's gone."

"Ouch," said Wood. "How long were you married?"

"No idea. Thirty-some... No, forty years, I think. I lost track."

"What happened?"

"We never got along, really. I thought she was mean, and she thought I was...emotionally distant. We just weren't suited."

"After forty years. Damn."

"It happens. In the last ten years we drifted apart."

"But you must once have been in love."

"I don't think so."

"No? Do you remember why you got married in the first place?"

"I don't know. She told me one day I was getting married and I said OK."

"Sounds like Monsieur Meursault."

"Who?"

"Meursault in *The Stranger*. His girlfriend says let's get married, and he simply doesn't care—it's meaningless to him—so he says OK."

I had read this book with many classes, but I had never noticed how closely my situation mirrored that of Meursault. I always portrayed Meursault as insane, a criminal, a misfit, but for a moment I had a twinge of sympathy for him. And for another moment I wished I'd be coming back next year to reread *The Stranger* as I had reread *Hamlet*.

"I recently discovered that Mrs. Kessler is in touch with my son," I said, "which really bothers me because I haven't heard from him in close to thirty years. Do you think I should try to contact Hank, my son?"

"Of course. How can you not have spoken to your son in thirty years? That's outrageous. The great failure of my life is that I have no children. Don't let your kid get away."

I resolved to contact Hank that night.

"If you don't call him, he will only hear Mrs. Kessler's side of the story."

"That's true... But what about Kay? Did you leave your wife for Kay?"

Wood remained reluctant. He examined his shoes for a moment, considering what to do, and when he looked up, he blushed. Then, seeing I was waiting for an answer, he began by saying, "Yes. I left Marie because I fell in love with Kay."

Fell in love! I thought. *Did he say 'fell in love'? Does that actually happen?*

Then Wood explained how, after the initial fervor of the affair, Kay had increasingly estranged herself from him, first sexually, then professionally, then as a drinking partner, and now, he feared, for good. "She told me a while ago," he said, "that the only reason she allowed me to have sex with her in the first place was that she felt sorry for me. How could she say that? The way I remember it, we were crazy about each other. And it was mutual. She may have cooled from the initial heat of the affair sooner than I, but we were totally in love at one time."

Now that Wood had got started, I feared where the conversation might go. I didn't want to hear a lot of baloney about Kay being in love, and I certainly didn't want to hear any of the details of Wood's sexual peccadilloes, especially if they concerned Kay.

"I actually begged Kay to leave her husband," he continued. "I wanted to marry her. But she refused. She was devoted to her daughter. I never stood a chance against her daughter. I finally found someone I wanted to be with, and she didn't want me. I think she felt toward me about the same way I felt toward Marie."

Love triangles, I thought. *The scourge of the very lucky.* But I stayed quiet, hoping Wood's rant would fizzle out. It didn't.

"In the beginning, Kay and I were friends. We shared a common lunch period, like you and I. And we found we had a lot in common. We both distrusted the school's administration and loved to criticize their incompetence. We both took the teaching job seriously. We shared ideas. Then we discovered we both had been a couple of sluts in college, and one thing led to another. Should have been simple. But, no. Once we had sex, and mixed sex with friendship, I was a goner."

Oh, dear, this is getting out of control, I thought. And I said, "The bell's about to ring." But Wood was on a tear.

"Does it sound like she was feeling sorry for me? I'm not sure how she felt, but I fell in love. Deeply and completely in love. At home, Marie was furious. She always knew when I was cheating. But I loved everything about Kay—her looks, her humor, her manners, the way she talked, the way she buttered her toast..."

"I really have to finish this sonnet before the bell rings," I said.

"...Then she cooled off, just like that—not before Marie was gone—but too soon. Last time we met, I asked her to remember the last time we were together, and do you know what she said? She said the whole affair was 'ridiculous.' That was her word to sum up our relationship: 'ridiculous.' 'It was completely ridiculous,' she said."

"That's a shame. Look—" I said.

Wood succumbed to his memories. "She was really something. You want to know how intense our relationship was? Well
for me anyway, it was all-consuming; she was my life. And now
she says it was ridiculous..." Was Wood on the verge of tears? He
was staring at nothing, glassy eyed.

"Oh my God," I said.

"What?" asked Wood, waking from his trance.

"Listen to the text on the page I have opened." I read from the
text in my hands: "Past cure I am, now Reason is past care, and
frantic-mad with evermore unrest; my thoughts and my discourse
as madmen's are..."

"Yes," said Wood. I—"

Mercifully the bell rang for dismissal and Wood desisted.

On our way back to class Wood said, enigmatically, "Never
give a narcissist a vibrator as a gift. You'll never see her again."

I was shaken for the rest of the week. It killed me that Wood
had had this relationship. Try as I might to moralize the situation,
to vilify Wood for seducing a married woman, the provocative
image of Kay overwhelmed my other thoughts, and my morality
evaporated. In class, I kept my eyes on the clock for the rest of the
week, wishing the hands would hurry and the silly week would
end. In the evening, I required an extra ounce or two of gin to
still my impatience for Friday. The sonnets offered solace but not
a cure. Was I becoming as crazy as Wood? I had only one chance
for a reprieve: that when we had drinks, Kay would turn out to be
boring or stupid. But I was disappointed.

On Friday, when Kay walked into the bar where Wood and I had
already begun to drink, she strode in with the confidence of the
most beautiful woman in the room—which she was. Seeing her,
I thought, *Wood should thank his lucky stars he'd slept with her
even once, instead of crying like a baby because she wouldn't
trot off to bed with him every day. What a spoiled man! I'd give
anything for an opportunity just to rest my hands on her hips,
and here's this Wood, who was lucky enough to have had a real
relationship with her, complaining!* I felt like giving Mr. Wood a
piece of my mind.

When Kay was close, I could see the crow's feet at the corner
of her eyes and the tiny cracks in her lips, and I was sure her chin
had once been better chiseled, but these marks of time failed to

diminish her essential beauty. She would be beautiful when she was eighty. Besides, she was a virtuoso storyteller, and she dominated the conversation from the moment she arrived, relegating her good looks to a secondary position.

Descending from his stool, Wood touched her side and kissed her cheek. Though we'd saved her a seat, she never sat but, to accentuate her stories, stood between our barstools and gesticulated like an actress on a stage.

"Unbelievable!" said Kay, "What a day I had! You're not going to believe this."

"Kay," said Wood, "you remember Arnold Kessler."

I had no idea how to behave in the presence of such a beauty, a woman who smelled so expensive and wore a tailored jacket that accentuated her shape. I thought: *Shake her hand—no; kiss her cheeks—no; jump down from the stool, grab her in your arms, kiss her lips...no.* I smiled vaguely and nodded. She was used to meeting flustered men and touched my knee to put me at ease. "Nice..." she surveyed my clothing but couldn't find anything nice, so she pointed vaguely and said, "...something or other."

"What are you drinking?" asked Wood.

"I'll have a cosmo," said Kay, and she began a story as though she had already been telling it for an hour and we just happened by. "So. There's this woman in my department who was a nun before she became a teacher. And she lives in a state of constant moral indignation—can't believe what she's seeing. You know how Peale is. The kids are not what you'd call models of virtue, especially the basketball players. They're like privileged characters, treated like princes—like professional athletes. You know how athletes go around raping women and shooting up discos and they can get away with it because they're so beloved by all. Such local heroes. Well, the basketball players at Peale are the same way; you can see them in the hallway all day long when they should be in class, engaged in a kind of never-ending party of fast food and women and song—it's unbelievable... Are we getting something to eat? I'm starved... So where was I?"

"A woman who used to be a nun," said Wood. The barman supplied Kay with a pink martini, and, taking it, she incorporated the drink into her performance. Wood then huddled with the barman and ordered the infamous Provincial Sampler.

"Oh, yeah, the nun, Miss Douglass. You should see how this

woman dresses. I know she was a nun, but come on. She looks like she's Amish. Wears granny dresses down to here and a bun in her hair up to here. I don't know where she gets this stuff—she has to make it herself. The other day she wore a belt made of the same fabric as her dress. When was the last time you saw that? Anyhow, Miss Douglass doesn't complain, and she works hard, but you can see on her face that she is annoyed by what is going on around her—the moral turpitude. She's what our friend Mr. Kessler here would call *ungebluzen*. Do I have that right, Arnie, *ungebluzen?* She's a sourpuss; she looks like she's pissed off all the time. And, when you come down to it, who wouldn't be, at Peale? I mean, the kids are out of control, the principal is a moron, and half the teachers are absent every day. It's a real nuthouse. Coglin—that's the principal—has decided she's better off if she stays in her office and delegates, since every time she wanders the hallways she realizes she's in way over her head; and if she were to try to solve some problem she sees, like kids sneaking out the front door, it would mean she'd have to spend a whole week concentrating on that problem while a million other problems went untended, and she would probably fail to solve the original problem to anyone's satisfaction, including her own, and all she would have achieved is that she would have further proved her incompetence and not finished any of the paperwork she has accumulating on her desk. So she stays in her office, with her back to the door. There are teachers who say they've never seen her—don't know who she is. And maybe that's a good thing. Plus, she smells like cat piss, at least I hope it's cat piss; she is a cat lady... Where was I? I need another drink." Kay knew her way around a martini.

"A nun with a bun, a basketball player, a belt..." Wood turned to the barman.

"Oh, yes. You're not going to believe this. Miss Douglass, in her flowery nun's habit—that's what her dresses look like, nuns' habits with flowers or paisleys or God-knows-whatall—anyhow, she approached me last week, and she was looking particularly *ungebluzen*, and she asked me to come with her to the ladies' room. I couldn't imagine what was bothering her. She was really distraught, and I was hoping it wasn't some kind of woman's issue, because I really do not want to relate to this woman on that level. I mean, she probably doesn't want to destroy her virginity with tampons, and God knows what she's using for feminine hygiene.... She looked very somber, very upset, as she led me into the ladies' room, and she brought me right into one of the stalls, and I was freaking out by now, because she wouldn't say what the matter was, just led me into a stall...."

The barman brought the Provincial Sampler and set it on the bar, but when Wood invited Kay to partake, she said, "No, thanks, I'm not eating. I have a weekend down the shore coming up. So where was I?"

Wood and I took a cracker each and began to spread cheese. As though he'd had plenty of experience as Kay's prompter, he said, "*Ungebluzen*... ladies' room... stall..."

"Oh, yeah, you're not going to believe this. When we crowded into the stall together, Miss Douglass pointed down, and there was this huge turd in the toilet. Miss Douglass pointed to it and didn't say anything at first, and I didn't know what to think. I mean, was she trying to show me her shit? (Kay said this a bit too loud and put her hand over her mouth for a moment, looking around the bar guiltily, then proceeded in a quieter tone.) She was pointing to this turd and she was almost crying, poor dear. I looked at her, with her bun on her head, and her dollar-store half-glasses, and her dress from the Amish Salvation Army, and her eyes were getting all glassy and pink, and I didn't know what to say. I took another look at the shit, and there didn't seem to be anything wrong with it. It was normal enough—perhaps a bit larger than I might expect from the pious ass of Miss Douglass—but I couldn't figure out what the problem was...."

Wood and I were about to indulge in our crackers spread with pâté when Kay first spoke the word "turd" and, simultaneously, we set our crackers down on the plate to wait for a less graphic part of the story.

Kay was undeterred. "...'Miss Douglass,' I asked, 'why have you led me to the lavatory to show me your defecation?' and she wept and said, 'It's not mine.'" Kay placed her hand on her chest, just atop the lovely crease, to show her disbelief, and she took a generous slug of the pink concoction in her martini glass and continued, "And she told me the shit belonged to a student by the name of Yelps, who happens to be the captain of the basketball team. I asked her what she was talking about, and she came out with the story, 'As I was entering the ladies' room here,' Douglass said, 'Christian Yelps came out of this stall. So I asked him what he was doing in the teachers' restroom, and he said something about making a mistake and going through the wrong door, and he ran away. Then I opened the door of the stall, and this is what I found.' And I swear she was crying when she told me this. So I tried to calm her down by reminding her what terrible manners our students have, and how rude it was of Christian not to flush, and that I'd bring this incident to the attention of the basketball coach. The basketball coach is the only person who has control over these guys. He knows them intimately. I think he brings them home to live in his house. I know he bails them out of jail if they end up there. He's like their parent in absentia. They're each about seven feet tall, and huge, and he feeds them a special diet for lunch—out of his own pocket—so I know that the right guy to go to for this incident is the coach. But no! Douglass says she's going to go straight to the principal. She's going to write a pink slip and hand it directly to Coglin. And she goes on about how the incident is so egregious, and so symbolic, and how students are just "messing all over the school." And there was nothing I could do to prevent her from pursuing this thing. I thought it was one of those incidents where no one got hurt, no harm no foul, and the coach would know what to do to prevent future incidents. Besides, how could she describe an incident like this on a pink slip? But what could I do?"

"I think Miss Douglass had the right approach," I said.

"Why aren't you guys eating?" asked Kay. "It's not like Roger to refrain from eating." And here Kay reached through Wood's jacket and pinched his belly. "Damn, Rog, you're getting fat! But how about you?" Kay took an olive from the plate, bit half, and pointed it at me, "Why don't you eat something?"

Wood came to my defense and said, "Kessler here has recently lost sixty pounds."

"Oh," said Kay, placing the uneaten half of her olive back on the plate, "an anorexic. Eat something!" she commanded. And she commenced with her story, "Well, Douglass somehow described the incident on the pink slip, and the principal suspended Christian for shitting in the teachers' toilet, and today was the day that he and his mom came in to face the music. Since I'm the department chair, I was invited to attend the meeting, and so was the basketball coach. So here was Christian and his mom, who brought along Christian's little sister, a cute little thing in pigtails, and me and Miss Douglass, who outdid herself by actually wearing a cameo to button the top of her blouse, and the principal and the basketball coach all huddled around this pink slip Douglass had written in which she accused Christian of shitting in the wrong pot. And you had to be there to believe what happened. Christian's mother decided to play the part of a defense attorney, and she was a real firecracker, all six feet seven of her, a huge woman. She stood and aimed her questions right at poor, uptight Miss Douglass, 'How do you know that it was Christian's shit? Did it have his name on it? Can you tell whose shit belongs to who? Are you some kind of shit expert?' And Douglass was flummoxed. She didn't know what to say because she just wasn't used to this kind of language, and she started to hyperventilate. I thought she was going to die. And Christian himself was laughing himself silly which, by the way, made me want to laugh, though I was discreet, and I was very worried about Douglass, sitting there trying to control her breath. And Coach Steiner tried to get Christian to stay quiet by threatening to bench him, but Christian said, 'You know you can't bench me.' And in this confusion, Principal Coglin took the role of prosecuting attorney and tried to reason with Mrs. Yelps, saying the circumstantial evidence of Christian leaving the stall was all that was necessary to convict him. But Mrs. Yelps wasn't having any of that circumstantial stuff. She said, 'Do you have the shit? Did you save the shit? How do we know there was any shit in the first place?' To which I responded, 'I saw the shit. Miss Douglass showed me the shit.' But Mrs. Yelps persisted, "But couldn't it have been someone else's shit? Couldn't it have been Miss Douglass's own shit?' And she pointed—accusingly—at Douglass, who was choking but managed to say, 'I don't do those things.' And Mrs. Yelps said, 'Be-scuse me, you don't shit?' And this brought the house down. Everyone but Douglass had to laugh. We were dying—especially Christian, who fell on the floor, all seven feet of him, while Douglass said, 'No, I mean I never forget to flush.'"

Wood and I joined Kay in a laughing fit. She touched both our knees and said, "Wait. Wait. Here comes the kicker: When we settled down, Mrs. Yelps actually said, 'I have a character witness I'd like to call." She said that: 'a character witness I'd like to call,' as though she were an actual attorney. We were stunned. And she called Christian's little sister over from where she was playing with a sock monkey she had brought with her. So here was this little kid with pigtails and a sock monkey standing on the principal's carpet, and we were all looking at her and her mother asks her, 'Shay-shay,' or 'Nay-nay' or whatever, 'Does your brother Christian sometimes go to the bathroom to make a poo poo?' And the kid says, 'Yeth,' just like that, 'Yeth.' And mom says, 'Have you ever gone into the bathroom after Chris has made a poo poo?' 'Yeth.' And then mom lowered the boom, 'Have you ever, ever, known of a time when Chris did not flush the toilet?' And the kid says, 'No, Chris flushes.' And mom says, 'I rest my case.'"

Here Kay hesitated and sipped her drink, as though the story were ended. "What happened to Chris?" asked Wood.

"I don't know. The principal asked Christian to apologize to Miss Douglass, which scandalized Mrs. Yelps, but Chris was encouraged by Coach Steiner to accept this as a kind of plea bargain. And Chris made a half-hearted apology, which made Miss Douglass burst out crying and leave the room. And that was the end."

Wood and I resumed eating the Provincial Sampler, but I was distracted suddenly when Kay leaned toward me and pressed her body against my knee. She was holding her glass up to get the barman's attention. The softness of her body ran through my bloodstream like hot soup on a cold day. I felt a stirring in my pants, and I think Kay noticed it, as though she had a sixth sense for such things. She leaned closer, my confusion obviously amusing to her. "I had a similar experience a couple of months ago," I said, "where I was down in the disciplinarian's office with a kid and his mother—" Kay touched my knee and looked in my eyes, probably to see if I could string words together while enthralled. I faltered. "I have this kid who is, who does, well, everything he does is—"

"No, wait, wait. Hold that thought, Arnie, " Kay took her drink from the bar. "Listen to this. I sent a diamond ring back to France after twenty years."

"Whose diamond ring?" asked Wood. I was glad I didn't have to tell the story about Augustus Merriwether, though it was apt. Kay was unwilling to cede any of the barroom entertainment to anyone who might be less amusing, and she understood in her storyteller's heart that she was saving me from myself.

"When I was traveling around France," Kay resumed, "years ago. I must have been about twenty-five—and I was staying in a kind of *pension* in Biarritz. Very nice place, close to the beach. And I was looking around the pension for a pen to write a post-card... I had been invited to spend the afternoon on a boat, or I should say the yacht, of a young Frenchman, me and some others from the pension, and I opened the drawer of a chest in the foyer, and there was this pretty little ring, like a wedding band, made of white gold, with three small diamonds in it, and I took it. I stole it. I don't know why I'd do such a thing. But I put it in the breast pocket of the shirt I had over my bikini and kept it there until I got back to my room and put it in my suitcase. I had never done such a thing, and I never have since... I took it home with me. But once I was back in the States and I unpacked it I was consumed by guilt. I couldn't believe I'd stolen someone's stuff."

"Wait a minute," said Wood, "I've seen you steal all kinds of things. Didn't you once heist a roll of the vice principal's craft paper, and how about the printer you took home for three years, and—"

"Alright already! That's different. Those are not thefts; they're school-related loans—the proper reallocation of supplies, putting them in places where they can be better used. And I eventually brought everything back—well, not the paper. If I recall, I gave the paper to you, you jerk. But this was different. This was someone's stuff, a ring that fit on someone's finger, a wedding ring, for Chrissake, with sentimental value. I couldn't believe I'd taken it. So I gave it to my mother, and I told her I'd bought it at a thrift store. And she loved it. She had it appraised and it was worth a few thousand dollars, which made me even more guilty. I mean, what kind of karma must I have racked up by stealing someone's ring and pawning it off on my mother with a lie—sticking my own mother with stolen goods. How many Japanese tourists would I have to consent to photograph, how many little kids would I have to give presents to, to counteract this bad karma? But after I gave it to my mother, I forgot about it. Until last month! Last month my mother gave the ring back to me, saying she doesn't wear it anymore, and I thought 'Aghhhh! It's back!' and I was racked by guilt again, only now it was doubled. The ring sat on my dresser and accused me of thievery every time I looked at it. It was driving me nuts. So I wrapped it up, and I put it in a box and sent it to the chief of police in Biarritz, with a little note telling the story. I sent it back. I was careful to put the right amount of postage on the box and drop it in a mailbox near school so the Biarritz police couldn't trace it back to me...."

"I'll bet the chief's wife appreciates your effort," I said.

"Don't say that," said Kay, and she pushed my arm, causing me to spill a sip or two of martini. "I've been having a stretch of misfortune for a few months," she said, and drank.

Wood raised his glass, "Balzac said, 'We exaggerate misfortune and happiness alike. We are never as bad off or as happy as we say.'"

"Oh, fuck off," said Kay. "Always with the Frog Lit."

Hear, hear! I thought. *I like this gal.*

Kay took a break. There was an open place next to Wood, and she grabbed Wood's jacket and tugged him off his seat as she told him to move over so she could sit between us. Seated, nearing the bottom of her third drink, Kay complained, "It started with the transmission in my car. Cost a fortune to fix, and it's still a little funky. Then, Jess, my daughter (Kay clarified for my benefit), applied to Brown, where she wanted to go, and got waitlisted. So that's up in the air. I think she'll be going to Penn State. Which is not what we wanted, though I would save a few bucks. And then that damned stock market dipped so low I lost half the money in my annuity. And listen to this, my goddamned husband hired a guy to refinish the stairs in my house, and the guy said he had a revolutionary new way to strip the finish on stairs, because apparently stairs are difficult to strip and—ya gotta hear this one—the guy poured some kind of flammable liquid on the stairs and lit it on fire and, whoosh, the flames flew up the stairs and set the house on fire—yes, the stairs and the walls and the balustrade were on fire! We called 911 and a fire truck came down the street, but by the time they came, the refinishing guy had taken off his shirt and pants and smothered the fire, and he was standing in our living room in his boxers, all blackened from head to toe...." Kay took a moment to drink. "By the way," here Kay turned toward Wood and spoke to him confidentially, though I heard her say, "I brought up that issue I told you about with my gynecologist—you remember?"

Wood said, "Oh, yeah, what did he say?"

"What did she say."

"OK, what did she say?"

"She told me to find a new boyfriend." Kay laughed.

Wood flushed, "Great. Thanks."

"Ah, well, *les grandes aventures amoureuses commencent par Champagne et terminent avec le tisane.*"

Kay said this loud enough for me, so I bit, "What's that?"

Wood answered, "She's quoting Balzac! Can you believe it—"

"Oh, too bad!" said Kay, and she grew quieter. "But the worst of it is my father. I have visited him every day after school. Every day. We can't get him to eat. He refuses. It's as though he wants to skip the last part of his life."

"Where is he? What happened?" I asked.

"He's in the rehabilitation center across from Nazareth Hospital. He had a stroke, and they said he needs a pacemaker. But he refused the operation. Now he's just not... thriving. He's getting sicker. And now he refuses to eat." Kay lost all vestiges of humor. She supported her forearms on the bar and looked down.

"How old is he?" I asked

"Seventy-nine. I don't think he'll live to be eighty."

"You should have made him get that pacemaker," said Wood.

"No!" Kay said emphatically. "I respected his wishes."

"What are they doing for him?" I asked.

"There's not much they can do except feed him with a tube. It looks like he's on life support. When I visit him he doesn't talk much, just nods. He's a skeleton. It's killing me."

Kay peered into her martini glass, and then downed the dregs. Staring straight ahead, she looked a little older, now that her performance was in intermission, more like the heroine of a country and western song than Shakespeare's Dark Lady. "I'm on my way to visit him now," said Kay, "back to the Northeast. What a cultural wasteland Northeast Philadelphia is. So depressing. Can shopping at strip malls be considered an art form, because it's the only art form practiced in the Northeast. I think it's the worst neighborhood in the city. Where are you from, Kessler?"

"Overbrook Park."

"Oh, I take that back. There are worse."

"We'll come with you to visit your father," said Wood.

Kay slid off her stool, "You don't have to. It's not what I'd call a Friday night's entertainment."

"No. We'll give you some moral support. You'll come, right Arnold?"

"Yeah, sure," I said, regretting it as I said it. It was in the opposite direction from home.

"No, really," said Kay.

"We want to go," said Wood, "Right, Arnie?"

"Absolutely," I said.

Before leaving the bar, we made arrangements to meet Kay in the lobby of the rehabilitation center, which would be easy to find since it was right on the Boulevard. "Who's paying?" asked Kay.

"Should we split?" I foolishly asked.

Kay put me in my place. "If you want to have drinks with this," Kay indicated her anatomy with gesture, "you don't split. Where'd you find this guy, Rog?"

"I'll get the check," said Wood, taking some bills from his pocket.

"That's better. I'll get the tip," said Kay, plucking a bill from Wood's hand and putting it on the bar. She scowled at me, "Split! Oh, brother." And she strode toward the door saying, "I guess that's how they do it in Overbrook Park." But I was busy admiring the way her short jacket fit as she pulled it into place and walked to the door. Wood caught me checking out Kay and gestured with his head that we should follow.

19. Kay's dad

PEOPLE—notably Mrs. Kessler—have said of me that I lack emotion, but I'm sure you have noticed that this is not true: I am perfectly capable, for example, of feeling jealousy—as evinced by my relationship with Wood. And I am quite prone to feelings of shame—and fear, too. You will recall that I was ashamed of myself when I broke my computer, and afraid. Shame followed me after Latovick accused me of cheating, and fear too. And I was consumed by shame and cowered with fear after I called Gus that dirty name. If shame and fear are my conscience's way of training me not to indulge in certain behaviors, then they're not working very well, since I have not become less fearful or less ashamed of myself with age. This is especially true of shame. If anything, I'm more ashamed of myself than ever. I embarrass myself all the time, and often I proceed to say or do something as shameful as the thing that caused me shame in the first place. It's a real shame. In any event, what Mrs. Kessler often said about me, that I feel no emotions, simply isn't true. I'm very emotional. I say all this because the next part of the story proves this. It is so embarrassing and shameful it's difficult to admit. Only my promise to myself to tell the truth, in the spirit of confession, allows me to continue.

As I drove up I-95 to meet my friends in the lobby of Kay's father's rehabilitation center, I entertained two conflicting thoughts. One was that I did not want to visit an old, sick person to top off my Friday night, and the other was that I didn't mind spending a while longer with Kay, even if it meant enduring the unfortunate circumstances of grieving over a sickbed. Her touch was still warm on my knee, and I thought I might be able to put my hands on her—on her shoulder, or possibly her waist—to comfort her in her grief.

I figured Kay was finished with Wood. She hardly spoke with him in the bar, and when she did exchange words, it seemed to be a confirmation that she had lost her feelings for him. Meanwhile, she had leaned her soft body against my leg and pushed me around a bit to enliven her performance, and these things, I reasoned, were indications that she wanted to get closer to me. Why else would she flirt with me? She might be beset by personal problems now, but once she was past this rough patch, she'd be back in the world of the living—looking, perhaps, for love; and who knows, I might be the guy. I was single, after all.

The sex fantasies I'd been having about Kay since I'd met her were usually interrupted by the presence of Wood or Mrs. Kessler, whose presence instantly popped the bubble of the fantasy. As I drove to the rehabilitation center, the fantasy I succumbed to was no exception. It involved Kay and me in a motel room. I have no idea why I plotted the fantasy in a motel room, since I lived alone and didn't need a motel room, but there we were. I imagined that she disappeared into the bathroom and reemerged wearing a see-through nightie—and she looked fantastic. As usual though, Wood popped up, sitting on a chair next to the dresser, where he sat toothpicking his lunch from his teeth. So I reimagined the scenario in a hurry, sending Kay back into the bathroom to change into a very frilly garter belt and an equally frilly bra, which looked a bit extreme. Kay, critical even in my fantasy, emerged from the bathroom and questioned the costume with an expression that said "Really?" I argued that it was, after all, my fantasy, and she conceded. I looked over to make sure Wood was gone, and he was. Mrs. Kessler was nowhere in sight, so I waved Kay toward the bed. Her black hair made a striking complement to her black lingerie, and everything was going fine in the fantasy, until Kay sat on the edge of the bed and I unhooked her bra. Abruptly, she changed her mind about the whole rendezvous, saying something about how "unacceptable" my bald head was, and held her bra stubbornly in place. She was angry with me, and she rehooked her bra, saying it was blasphemy to engage in this kind of behavior while her father lay on his sickbed. I spent the rest of the fantasy begging Kay to reconsider while she put her clothes back on.

When I arrived at the rehabilitation center, Kay was standing by a vending machine munching a PayDay candy bar. From the appearance of her mascara, she'd been crying, and Wood stood behind her murmuring soothing words, which I could not hear, but were probably some of those annoying quotes from Émile Zola.

We formed our group and went up the elevator to Mr. Fortunata's room. Elevator rides are so long when the riders are silent, as we were. Only flat-out platitudes occurred to me, and most likely to Wood also. I mean, what can you say that's original in this situation? "I'm sure your dad will be fine," or "Buck up, sweetheart"? Anything would sound stupid, and I didn't want to sound stupid...though I wished Wood would try.

In Mr. Fortunata's unit, there was a commotion at the nurse's station, and the staff was responding to an emergency somewhere on the floor. One nurse was giving orders in a decisive way to two other nurses, and then they spread out in different directions. We followed Kay to her father's room. When we entered the room, Mr. Fortunata was alone—the other bed was empty—and Kay ran to her father's bedside and asked, "What's happened?" Then she turned to us and said, "They've tied him down," and she turned back to her father to find out why.

He did not look good. I was expecting something grim, but not this. He was devoid of color, like a dead man, and so thin and frail it seemed unnecessary to tie his arms to his sides with wide belts. His stroke seemed to have immobilized him. He did not even open his eyes when he spoke. He said, feebly, from one corner of his mouth, "They're... force-feeding me." He had a feeding tube taped to his nose, along with an oxygen tube under his nose. There was an IV in his arm, along with various sensors coiled all around him to monitor his vital signs. I'm no expert, but when I read the monitor that showed his heartbeats, it appeared to be registering a measly forty-some beats a minute, and not too steadily either. It looked to me like this old gent's jig was up.

Kay said, "I'll speak to the nurse about this," though she knew the nurses were busy just then, and there was really nothing to be done for a while. She stood nervously and bit her lip.

"I'm...fine," whispered Mr. Fortunata. His head rolled toward us slightly, though his eyes remained shut. "I just want to go home."

"Why aren't you eating, Dad?" asked Kay. Her tears resumed.

Mr. Fortunata didn't answer, just nodded slightly. Then he seemed to have died. He lay perfectly still and white as his sheets, though the monitor showed his ticker was still running, but just barely.

"You'll be hungry in a couple of days, Dad," said Kay, dabbing her eyes. She touched her father's shoulder.

"No," said Mr. Fortunata, "I've had it." His voice trailed off, and he began to breathe heavily. The monitor showed a heart rate of forty-eight beats per minute. He mumbled, "I'm finished... eating."

Kay turned toward Wood and buried her head in his shoulder. He put his arm around her, and she abandoned herself to her grief. "He doesn't want to live anymore," she said between sobs. "He hasn't eaten since the stroke."

A slow, quiet rattle came from Mr. Fortunata's throat. "Please," he said, quieter than the buzz of the lights.

I have no idea what made me think I could help old Mr. Fortunata. Perhaps it was an attempt to impress Kay as she leaned toward Wood for solace, or perhaps I simply felt the need to be a Good Samaritan. In any event, while Wood intoned a sympathetic *"Shhhh"* to the distraught Kay, I decided the restraints on the old guy's arms were an unnecessary annoyance for him. He was too weak to do any mischief in his condition, and they looked too tight. So I undid the restraint that was closest to me and, when Mr. Fortunata did not suddenly rear up in rebellion and try to escape, I leaned over to undo the other restraint. I was trying to make the old guy more comfortable. The second restraint, however, was less cooperative, and when I tried to loosen the belt, it didn't give, but instead, it pulled me off balance, and I found myself falling on top of the old man. Kay looked around from Wood's shoulder and gasped, but she gasped even louder when I tried to break my fall onto Mr. Fortunata with my free arm, and I accidentally snagged his nasal feeding tube with my fingers. This yanked the tube halfway up his esophagus, causing him to make a scary guttural noise, like *"Agh-aghh,"* and then he started to choke.

"Oh God," said Wood, in a panic. "I'll go and get a nurse," and he flew out of the room. Kay was equally shocked, and she sobbed, but the remedy to the situation seemed simple enough to me. I proceeded to push the feeding tube back into Mr. Fortunata's nose and down his throat. But this operation was trickier than I thought, and he kept bobbing up and saying *"Agh—agh—agh—"* and choking weakly as I fumbled. So I just pulled the damn thing out quickly, as one would pull a Band-Aid off a wound. The old man's eyes opened wide, but he was too stunned to make a sound.

Kay raised her hands to her mouth and groaned, "This is not happening."

I didn't realize the feeding tube would keep pumping out its nutritional goo, and when it squirted, I didn't know what to do with it, so I let it drop to the floor and turned toward Kay to apologize. She took a step backward and looked at me like I was some kind of a ghoul, her fists against her cheeks, though I distinctly heard the old man say, "Thank God!"

"He'll be fine," I said.

Then we learned why Mr. Fortunata had been restrained. He reached over to the IV needle in his arm and pulled it out, which got Kay's attention. "No, Dad!" she exclaimed. But it was too late. Blood began flowing from the hole in Mr. Fortunata's arm. Then he started peeling off the electrodes that were stuck to his chest, heedless to the scary amount of blood that was dripping from his arm onto the sheets and even onto the floor. "Don't worry, Dad!" screamed Kay, not knowing what to do, "Help is on the way!" The old man's heart monitor, deciding he was dead when he detached the electrodes, began to wail like an air raid siren, and flash. The wailing filled the room and the hallways. When I turned to see what was going on, I slipped on a puddle of goo, or blood, or both, that was accumulating on the floor, and I fell toward the edge of the bed. This time, when I tried to break my fall by grabbing whatever I could, I snagged the plastic catheter tube that hung by the side of the bed and pulled it out of the poor old man. He folded like a lawn chair. I heard him say something like "Gak!" as I hit the floor. Then he lay down on his bed, supine and motionless, as though he were dead. Kay stood frozen, sobbing, saying, "Oh, oh, oh" after each of my unfortunate accidents. Urine poured freely onto the floor and mixed with blood and nutritional goo. And I lay in it, on my back, wondering if I'd hurt myself. Kay stepped backward, avoiding the spill and, perhaps above all, avoiding me.

Trying to get back on my feet, I flopped around in this ungodly mess, but it was too slippery, and I only managed to kick the brake lever on the wheels of the bed, propelling the bed into the stand that supported the vital-sign monitors, and they fell off their stand onto a chair. While I flailed on the floor, the monitors lay in a tangle on the chair and continued to wail and flash, announcing the death of old Mr. Fortunata, although the old guy was suddenly livelier than ever—he'd come to. He was leaning over to watch me wallow in the muck, and I swear he had a smile on his face.

I extended my hand to Kay for help, but she looked at me like I was the Creature from the Black Lagoon. I was tired and shaky, lying there, and my heart felt like it would register an easy one hundred and fifty beats per minute if it were attached to the fallen monitor, so I gave up and rested in the gooey puddle.

Then Kay stepped forward.

Now you might interpret what happened next as intentional on my part, but I insist it was not. It was completely accidental. Who wants to loll around in old-man urine? I needed help. When Kay was close enough, I grabbed her legs to use as a brace to lift myself up. "Hey, get offa me!" she cried, but I needed to lift myself out of the slough. She tried to pry me loose while I climbed up her legs and—inadvertently!—I found myself grasping her buttocks and drawing her toward me. She recoiled, but I was not about to fall back into the soup, so I continued to climb, and I inched my way up, until, somehow, my hands wandered around her waist, and one hand came to rest on her breast. I got back on my feet by grasping Kay's waist and clutching her breast—but it was not because I wanted to feel her up; I was just trying to stand.

She looked at me with an expression of profound revulsion— which probably had more to do with my vile smell than anything else—and, at the very moment when Wood and all three nurses entered the room, Kay shoved me away so hard I almost slipped down again. "You dumb fuck!" she screamed, her mascara in Rorschach designs and her mouth taut with anger. Then, while Mr. Fortunata clapped his hands and smiled with all the strength the bleeding man could muster, Kay hauled off, with surprisingly good form, and slugged me. A right-hand jab, right on the lip. Seeing blood, she balled both her fists and was about to rain blows on me, but Wood restrained her.

I ran. The emergency siren filled the hall, and I heard laughter and confusion in my wake, but I hurried directly to the parking lot without stopping. In an effort not to dirty my car, I removed my pants and shirt and put them in my trunk and, since I was not wearing a tee shirt, I drove home in just my boxers, shoes, and socks. It was terrible when I had to stop for a light and the people in the car next to mine saw an inexplicably naked middle-aged man with a bleeding fat lip.

There, I have told it, as best I could, without leaving anything out. And I want to assure all of those who have accused me of being emotionally wrongheaded or morally retarded or whatever, that I have felt the appropriate shame as a result of all this. On my way home, Disciplinarian Squires's assessment of me echoed inside my head:

"You always were a fuckup, Kessler."

20. Retirement

So THAT's the story. I'm done. There were two weeks left in the school year after that fateful Friday night, but I did not return to Northwest. Too embarrassed. I didn't want to answer questions about the fat lip, and I couldn't look Wood in the eye. So I took the rest of the semester off. I had plenty of days in my sick-leave bank, and I seriously doubted that the principal would make a fuss about my absence, so I bailed.

I did visit Northwest High one last time. I came to school very early that Monday morning to pack my things. And while I was there, I raided the department's supply closet, loading up a shopping bag full of three-by-five cards, Scotch tape, staples, and paper clips—enough to last the rest of my life. And then I went home and called in sick for the remainder of the year. (I accidentally filched a box of yellow highlighters, which I never use, so I gave them to kids on Halloween.)

It is customary for retiring teachers at Northwest to make a speech to their peers on the last day of the school year. The retiree modestly rises and thanks the administration for the privilege of having been allowed to teach "the leaders of tomorrow." Then he recounts some fond memories from years gone by and explains what he will do with the leisure time he has earned—golf, family, travel, whatever. Then the proud retiree receives a parting gift, a glass bowl or a watch or something, and the audience of

teachers applauds wildly. Everyone is all smiles. It's a very sentimental affair. And I was looking forward to making this speech,
because I was going to say a few things I always wanted to say.
First I was going to explain that my career as a teacher had been
nothing less than forty years of unadulterated hell, and I couldn't
remember the last time I didn't return home from work so sick I
felt like dying. I was going to say that, as far as I was concerned,
the kids were a lot of noisy malcontents who lived only to pro-
crastinate, and my colleagues (sitting before me and listening to
my speech) were nothing but a bunch of silly dreamers who were
naïve enough to think they had some effect on their students. And
I would end my speech by telling everyone, including the principal, that I was having the last laugh because I'd milked the system
and the retirement fund owed me a bundle after I did half the
work of everyone else.

But I planned that speech and wrote it out before the few
gratifying teaching experiences I had in my last few weeks. My
experiences with *Hamlet* and the Sonnets changed my mind and,
I have to say, made me feel ridiculous and not a little guilty about
ever having planned such a speech. Good thing I never made that
speech. It would have been yet another embarrassment.

As for Kay, I had a bit of trouble getting her off my mind. I
hoped that she could forgive me for any problems I may have
caused her father, and I wanted to see her again. Shortly after
the incident in the rehabilitation center, I sent her a text message. It took me the better part of an hour to figure out how to use
the text message function on my phone. Then it took me another
hour to settle on the message as I considered everything from "I
think I love you" to "What's up," and I finally settled on "Thinking of you." Then, after another hour of nervous deliberation over
whether to send the message or not, I closed my eyes, held my
breath, and pressed the send button.

Kay did not respond. After a week or so, I decided to pay her a
visit. I looked up her address on the Internet. Then I went downtown to where she lived, and knocked on her door. It was five-
thirty in the evening, so I thought she must be home. But she was
not. Her husband opened the door and said, "Yes?" He was a tall,
handsome sort of guy dressed in a white shirt and a striped tie,
and when he answered the door, I felt like a little kid who was
visiting a new friend for the first time and felt intimidated by the

parent who opened the door. I almost said, "Can Kay come out and play?" but I simply asked, "Is Kay home?" And when the tall, professional-looking man with the Hollywood five-o'clock stubble said "No" in an interrogative tone, I said "Thank you," and made a quick getaway. In my car, I realized that it was a good thing she was not home because I didn't really have any business with her beyond "Hello." I would have had nothing to say beyond "How's your dad?" And for that I might have gotten another shot in the lip. I only hoped I left her husband completely baffled by the little old bald guy who came looking for Kay. Otherwise she'd have some explaining to do.

A week later, I received a letter from a lawyer that said if I ever tried to contact Kay or come near her that I would become liable for a civil action and a possible criminal suit for sexual harassment. The legal firm on the letterhead had a dubious name—Diktat, Fleece, and Swagger—but I didn't try to find out if they were a real firm or not. Instead, I scuttled any plan to contact Kay. The last thing I needed was a sexual harassment suit. Something like that might jeopardize my pension. And besides it would please Mrs. Kessler entirely too much if I were to get into trouble. I could hear her now: *"I told you Arnie was crazy...I told you he was an Asperger..."* Besides this letter, I received a phone call from someone who sounded like a tough guy, and he told me the same thing as the lawyers—not to go near Kay—although he sounded a bit like an impersonator of Edward G. Robinson; he kept saying "see" after every sentence. But it didn't matter to me if the lawyer and the tough guy were real or not, I got the picture. I desisted— though they couldn't reach into my fantasy world and pull Kay out of there. In my fantasies she still cavorts in very lacy undies.

Summer passed. I holed up in my closet. The new school year began. One afternoon a few weeks ago I called Mr. Wood to find out what happened with my broken computer. We had a short conversation, and Wood was congenial. He did not allude to anything that might be construed as misconduct on my part the last time we were together, and I was grateful. He told me Mrs. Worthington was promoted to an administrative position, so she was not teaching any classes this year, and we both agreed that it was a shame that the best teachers often do not teach. Mr. Hegel, he said, had transferred to a vocational school, where we assumed the crafts he required as projects could only be even more elaborate, but at least there were no life-sized historical artifacts lying around the English office any more. Wood also told me that he had given up eating those wonderful sandwiches. "Not the sandwiches!" I exclaimed. He explained how he had broken off his relationship with Kay altogether, and he was now dating Miss Rigg, who introduced him to vegetarianism. It seems Miss Rigg took over my room and found herself in the same situation I found myself in the previous year—being supplanted during her lunch period by a floating teacher and having to eat lunch in the English office, where she was thrown together with Wood, and they hit it off. "So what are you eating for lunch?" I asked.

"A banana, an apple, and a snack bar," he said, "and thank God for the snack bar." We laughed. "I lost twelve pounds," he said.

"Aren't you robbing the cradle with Miss Rigg?"

"She's thirty-three," he said, though I never would have guessed it.

"Well, I think you two make a sweet, wholesome couple," I said, and I meant it. Wood's relationship with Kay, though it survived Peale High, was probably destined to fail.

I asked if he had heard from Kay, but he said he hadn't, although he had spoken with another old colleague from Peale, who said that my misadventures at the rehabilitation center had become prime material for Kay when she entertained the staff at teachers' meetings and after-school parties. According to this informant, I was becoming a legend at Peale on account of Kay's skillful rendering of that awful night. I suppose she also included my text messages and the visit, but Wood spared me the embarrassment of talking about those things if he knew about them.

"What happened to Mr. Fortunata?" I asked.

"The craziest thing. After you left, he made a miraculous recovery. In fact, after you ran away, he astonished everyone by saying, 'I'm hungry, what's for dinner?' But then he died a few weeks later."

Wood finished our conversation by telling me he returned my broken computer and the only consequence was a sour look from the technology person, who I guess was powerless at that point. When I said good-bye to Wood, I had the distinct feeling that I'd never hear from him again.

I regret losing the friendship of Mr. Wood. Though I was jealous of him, I liked him. Perhaps this was because he was, for a while, the only friend I'd had in ages. I really should call him again to explain about stealing his stories and apologize for that. But I'm afraid he might feel violated. When you think about it, though, it's really his own fault if someone retells his stories. He did not apply for a copyright or anything—he just put them out there— so they are not legally his. And I hope that he would understand that when I retired, I needed those stories. I had no plans. I had no friends. I belonged to no groups. I had nothing to do, except watch TV and drink martinis. His stories were my saving grace.

Because of Wood's stories, I wrote this memoir. As soon as I retired, I started transcribing and editing the stories I'd recorded in secret. And I found I depended on them to fill my empty hours. They were amusing and, in a way, very soothing—and something else—they were indicative of something...something biographical. I think the stories—especially the ones about nutty administrators—provided me with a rationale or an excuse for the way I conducted myself as a teacher throughout my career. Anyhow, when I finished editing Wood's stories, I had to confront my situation in retirement—whole days with nothing to do. I tried goofing off, but I missed my cozy writing closet where I worked for hours on Wood's stories. I was bored, and my cocktail hour kept inching its way closer and closer to breakfast. I soon ran back to my closet and racked my brain trying to think of something to write. For weeks, I wrote anything that came to mind—letters to the editor, philosophical essays (you should have seen those), prospective letters to Mrs. Kessler (even one in which I begged her to come home). But all of these writings were unsatisfying. I don't think I finished a single one. I even tried to invent some stories, just like Wood's, about Peale High, but I couldn't. Finally I embarked on this autobiographical project and...*voilà*. The first four drafts, which I have discarded, were studded with lies and evasions—I think it is a natural human instinct to rewrite history so it reflects favorably on the writer. I actually portrayed myself in one draft as an educational innovator who was beset by regressive forces beyond his control (I think I discarded that draft after a chapter and a half). But when I resolved to simply tell the truth, I finally felt like I was on to something, that I had something worthy enough to stand side-by-side with Wood's teacher tales. So the truth set me free, I guess.

And this brings us back to the present. I've been writing for quite a while this morning—trying to finish this memoir. The paisley-shaped flowers on the wallpaper in my closet are starting to revolve as gently as the gears of a clock, and that tells me it's time to wrap things up for today and go downstairs to say hello to my good friend Gordon. Funny thing. I always thought when I retired that my various illnesses would magically subside—that they were caused by the job of teaching, and if I didn't work, they would disappear. But I was wrong. Not only do I still suffer from all the maladies that plagued me throughout my career, I have fallen victim to a few new symptoms, notably a pain in my eye that just won't quit. I'll make an appointment with the doctor. Mrs. Kessler's health insurance will pay. That's fitting since she's probably causing the pain by sticking her voodoo-doll Mr. Kessler in the eye with a pin.

I still haven't contacted Hank. Gotta do that.

RICHARD ADELMAN is a lifelong resident of Philadelphia. He taught English, computer applications, and filmmaking in public high schools there for thirty-seven years. Besides teaching, Richard worked for many years in the Philadelphia area as a wedding photographer and in Atlantic City as a bartender and restaurant manager. He is previously unpublished. Retired now, he has been spending his literary efforts trying to learn enough French to read the classics. He has two grandchildren.

PHOTO: CHERYL FEDYNA

Acknowledgments

I would like to thank my friends Elayne Bloom and Mike Herr for reading early drafts of this novel and making important suggestions. A fine author from New Texture, Andy Biscontini, was first to see the potential of the book, after my son Jake, Andy's old friend, brought it to his attention. Thanks to both, and to Wyatt at New Texture for agreeing with Andy that the public would appreciate it. My French teacher, Julie Castagnet at the *Alliance Français de Philadelphie*, and Vanina Marsot, author of *Foreign Tongue* (www.vaninamarsot.com), helped with the French in Chapter 6. Without them, I would have made a fool of myself. Also, Lewis Sayre, MD, provided valuable information about intensive care apparatus and how it might be abused. My experience as a teacher at Bartram High School and Central High School in Philadelphia provided some of the source material for this book, so I'd like to thank everyone I knew in those two fine institutions. I'd even like to thank the School District of Philadelphia for hiring me back in the '70s, and keeping me employed for close to thirty-seven years. The pay was not great, but the pension is coming in handy. Finally, I need to thank Cheryl Fedyna, my friend and colleague, who often encouraged me to pursue literary objectives, and who, after reading a fair copy of the novel, while I waited with bated breath for her to finish, said, "I think you pulled it off," and I breathed a sigh of relief.

"**JOSH ALAN FRIEDMAN**
HAS THE CHOPS OF A WOLF."
– JERRY WEXLER

Jerry Leiber Doc Pomus Ronnie Spector
Dr. John Mose Allison Keith Ferguson

TELL THE TRUTH
UNTIL THEY BLEED

Fathead Newman Joel Dorn Tommy Shannon
Chuck Rainey Cornell Dupree Sam Myers
Rick Sikes & the Rhythm Rebels

WYATT
DOYLE
BOOKS

new texture

MORE TRUTH AT
BLACK CRACKER online.com

"TELL THE TRUTH

JOSH ALAN FRIEDMAN

UNTIL THEY BLEED"

PAPERBACK, EBOOK, AND LIMITED EDITION HARDCOVER

ERIC REYMOND

Volumes of Worlds

essays on Brooklyn, Kansas and Beyond

PAPERBACK, EBOOK, AND LIMITED EDITION HARDCOVER   # new texture

The Revolution will be on the Moon.

nu luna

Andrew Biscontini

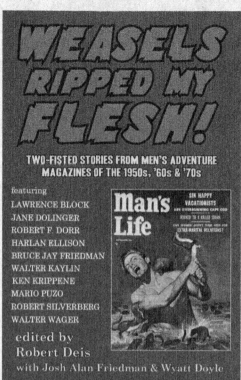

WEASELS RIPPED MY FLESH!

is an all-star powderkeg of two-fisted pulp fiction by some of the toughest writers to ever punch a typewriter. Return to a lost era of raw adrenaline, when every dame was a *femme fatale* and real men fought small mammals bare-handed. Hard-hitting stories and reminiscences by **Lawrence Block, Harlan Ellison, Bruce Jay Friedman, Walter Kaylin, Mario Puzo, Robert Silverberg** and more!

EDITED BY ROBERT DEIS WITH JOSH ALAN FRIEDMAN & WYATT DOYLE

HE-MEN, BAG MEN & NYMPHOS

rips the lid off the pulps' best kept secret, bringing **Walter Kaylin's** unique brand of tension and tough-guy thrills to a new generation of readers. Kaylin scaled new heights of ingenuity and invention in every genre, while setting the standard for the kind of unapologetic savagery and excess that made men's adventure magazines notorious—then and now. *Nymphos* hits like a clenched fist; get yours or get out of the way!

EDITED BY ROBERT DEIS & WYATT DOYLE

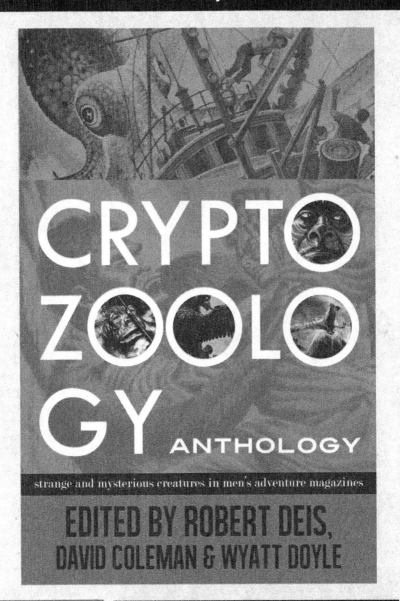

GET ON THE BUS.

STOP REQUESTED

WYATT DOYLE

ILLUSTRATIONS BY
STANLEY J. ZAPPA

"A wonderful addition to the literature of the lost and the doomed . . .
This is 21st Century America. Someone who wants to understand this
age 100 or 200 years from now should read this book. It's all here."
— Bill Shute, Kendra Steiner Editions

PAPERBACK, EBOOK, AND LIMITED EDITION HARDCOVER   # new texture

1965. Flashpoint of the Civil Rights Movement.

In every American city, interracial tensions threaten to boil over into violence.

And in Glen Cove, Long Island, Josh Friedman finds himself on the front lines of the fight for racial equality.

Josh is nine.

Race. Segregation. Doo-doo jokes.

BLACK CRACKER

an autobiographical novel
by Josh Alan Friedman

from WYATT DOYLE BOOKS

BLACK CRACKER online.com   # new texture

PAPERBACK, EBOOK, AND LIMITED EDITION HARDCOVER

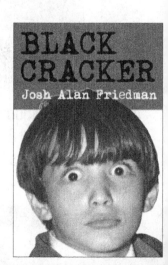

BOOKSELLERS

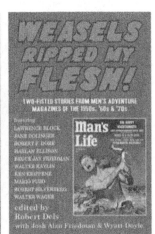

most

 # new texture

releases are available through Ingram

new texture

CPSIA information can be obtained at www.ICGtesting.com
Printed in the USA
BVOW08s1933240615

405859BV00001B/4/P

9 781943 444014